Leckie × Leckie
Scotland's leading educational publishers

D1766357

HIGHER
Chemistry

grade **booster**

Peter Uprichard ✕ Helen Stewart

Text © Peter Uprichard and Helen Stewart
Design and layout © 2009 Leckie & Leckie
Cover image © Naili Boratav/PBase.com

01/271109

ISBN 978-1-84372-722-4

Published by
Leckie & Leckie Ltd, 3rd floor, 4 Queen Street, Edinburgh, EH2 1JE
Tel: 0131 220 6831 Fax: 0131 225 9987
enquiries@leckieandleckie.co.uk   www.leckieandleckie.co.uk

Special thanks to
documen (design and page makeup),
Sandy Macfarlane (review),
Tara Watson (proofreading),
Rachel Wilkie (copy-editing).

A CIP Catalogue record for this book is available from the British Library.A CIP Catalogue record for this book is available from the British Library.

Leckie & Leckie makes every effort to ensure that all paper used in its books is made from wood pulp obtained from well-managed forests, controlled sources and recycled wood or fibre.

® Leckie & Leckie is a registered trademark
Leckie & Leckie Ltd is a division of Huveaux plc.

Acknowledgements
Leckie & Leckie has made every effort to trace all copyright holders.
If any have been inadvertently overlooked, we will be pleased to make the necessary arrangements.

We would like to thank the following for permission to reproduce their material:
SQA for permission to reproduce quotes and past examination case studies.

Every effort has been made to trace the copyright holders and to obtain their permission for the use of copyright material. Leckie & Leckie will gladly receive information enabling them to rectify any error or omission in subsequent editions.

Printed and bound by Martins the Printers, Berwick upon Tweed

CONTENTS

Introduction

WHAT THIS BOOK IS FOR

Welcome to your studies of Higher Chemistry! Whilst it is considered to be one of the more challenging courses, success at the end will be all the more rewarding. This book is designed to support the work you've done in class and to lead you step by step into a fuller understanding of the material covered and the way to get the best grade you can. There is no substitution for individual application and hard work, but we aim to give you the tools you need to answer competently and comprehensively and thereby to do the best you can.

You will have covered all the theory required in class, so this book will not revisit theory but rather provide you with a breakdown of the kind of answers you need to give in your exam to secure high marks.

It is impossible to cover every aspect of the course, so we will highlight the areas that we feel are of greatest importance, and the areas that are most likely to get you marks in your exam. We will focus on key areas where you can be trained to improve, such as calculations, PPA questions and problem solving.

HOW TO USE THIS BOOK

Interacting with learning material is a powerful way of obtaining feedback on your strengths and weaknesses. The content of this book will give you the opportunity to develop the different strategies necessary to handle the Higher examination questions. It will also help you to make the best use of what you know. Asking questions of your teacher is fundamental to improvement and confidence building, and so is something you should be doing regularly.

The aim of this book is to support your learning and give you an alternative source of information. It is not meant to be read continuously from cover to cover, although it would be good to have read and worked through the whole book by the end of the course. With experience, you will develop a self-awareness of those areas of weakness which require support (as well as others where you know you are doing well). These areas should guide you to the sections of this book where you most need extra assistance.

WHEN TO USE THIS BOOK

As with learning most things, the earlier you get started the better. Once you have started your course, you will very quickly meet questions that are typical of the National Examination and relevant to the material you are working on. Using this book simultaneously will be of great help. The structure of the course and the design of the examination are described below. Read up on these early on and come back to refresh your memory. As the formal school and National Examinations come closer, use this book more intensively to help you understand the typical structure of questions and how best to tackle them. Your aim is to have specific skills which can be transferred to different contexts, making the best of what you have learned.

COURSE DESIGN AND ASSESSMENT

You can find very precise details about the layout of the Higher Chemistry course by visiting the Scottish Qualifications Authority (SQA) website at www.sqa.org.uk. This will take you to a home page where you select the subject 'Chemistry'. You are allowed to print out anything here provided it is not used for any purpose other than for your own use as a student. The outline of the course design detailed below is based on the information on this website.

The Higher Chemistry course is divided into three units:

- Unit 1 Energy Matters

  This unit covers the following topics:

  a. Reaction rates

  b. Enthalpy

  c. Patterns in the Periodic Table

  d. Bonding, structure and properties

  e. The mole

  The Planning, Preparation and Assessment (PPA) topics covered in this Unit are:

  1. Effect of concentration on the rate of reaction

  2. Effect of temperature on the rate of reaction

  3. Enthalpy of combustion.

- Unit 2 The World of Carbon

  The Unit covers the following topics:

  a. Fuels

  b. Nomenclature and structural formulae

  c. Reactions of carbon compounds

  d. Uses of carbon compounds

  e. Polymers

  f. Natural products

  The PPAs covered in this Unit are:

  1. Oxidation

  2. Making esters

  3. Factors affecting enzyme activity

- Unit 3 Chemical Reactions

  This Unit covers the following topics:

  a. The chemical industry

  b. Hess's law

  c. Equilibrium

  d. Acids and bases

  e. Redox reactions

  f. Nuclear chemistry

  The PPAs covered in this Unit are:

  1. Verification of Hess's law

  2. Quantitative electrolysis

  3. Redox titration

When each unit has been completed it is assessed internally. This consists of a NAB test lasting 45 minutes and is worth 30 marks. In order to pass the NAB you have to score 18 or more marks.

THE EXAM

The National Examination lasts for 2 hours and 30 minutes and has 2 sections totalling 100 marks.

Section A:	40 multiple-choice questions.	40 marks
Section B:	Structured questions requiring written answers.	
	In this section approximately 6 marks are based on questions directly related to any of the nine PPAs.	60 marks

Of the 100 marks, approximately 60 marks are allocated to Knowledge and Understanding (KU) and the other 40 marks to Problem Solving (PS).

Knowledge and Understanding (KU)

Chemistry is a knowledge-based subject, and you will be expected to retain and understand information that you have been given in class. This is reflected in the bias of the marks allocated in both sections of the National Examination. For KU, you will need to be able to recall and recognise important facts and principles. The course is extensive and you must avoid compartmentalising your knowledge.

In other words, information on one topic will often need to be used to explain or understand what is happening in another context. For example, understanding the concepts of equilibrium learned in Unit 3 may well be required to fully understand the Chemical Industry topic. Only by practice and reflection will you develop the ability to see connections between different parts of the course.

Problem Solving (PS)

This is a section of the work which many students find difficult. It requires you to apply the knowledge and understanding that you have acquired to new situations. The best way to become adept at these questions is through practice.

In problem solving questions, you are required to be able to:

- complete diagrams of chemical apparatus
- answer questions based on flow diagrams
- interpret unfamiliar information
- analyse and interpret investigative techniques which are not in the Higher course

As said above, the best way to improve your problem-solving abilities is through practising these kinds of questions. Practice papers will be invaluable here and will help to prepare you for the way these questions are structured. Working through practice papers methodically and flagging up any areas of weakness will help you develop the specific skills you need to get the best possible marks. It is important always to answer problem-solving questions fully and not to take short cuts; marks can easily be lost by careless errors and insufficient attention to detail.

WHAT YOU SHOULD ALREADY KNOW

The S5 Higher Chemistry course builds very neatly on to the work you will have covered in S3 and S4, and so it is vital that you bring with you into your Higher studies some of the skills you already have. However, there are definitely areas of your previous studies that will prove more relevant. In a nutshell, you need to be comfortable and competent in the following areas:

- writing chemical formulae
- calculations
  - O calculations from balanced equations
  - O volumetric calculations

- reactions of acids
- basic organic chemistry
  - drawing organic structures
  - naming organic compounds from structures
- chemical reactions
  - neutralisation
  - precipitation
  - displacement/redox

We will not be covering the above topics in this book, but recommend that you revise these areas before embarking on the new Higher work. If you are finding a particular area difficult then you must read your notes, practise questions and ask your teacher. A solid foundation will be invaluable in your comprehension of the more difficult theory you will be covering in S5.

AREAS OF DIFFICULTY

Each year, the Principal Assessor for the SQA produces a list of areas where candidates have experienced difficulty in answering questions. Here is a collection of these over a period of about five years, listed under their respective unit titles.

Unit 1 Energy Matters

Enthalpy of neutralisation calculations

Bonding and structure

Intermolecular forces

Avogadro calculations

PPAs – effect of concentration on reaction rate;
            effect of temperature on reaction rate

Unit 2 The World of Carbon

Isomers

Oxidation of alcohols

PPAs – preparation of an ester;
            action of enzymes

Unit 3 Chemical Reactions

Ion-electron equations

Redox reactions

Equilibrium

Faraday calculations

PPAs – Hess's Law;
   electrolysis;
   redox titration

It would therefore make sense for you to prioritise the above areas when preparing for your exam. It is always easier to work on areas you are comfortable with; much more beneficial, however, is to work on areas you find challenging!

CHEMICAL REAGENTS

The Higher course requires you to know a number of chemical reagents, when they are used and the colour changes associated with them. The following table contains some of the common reagents you will meet.

Reagent	Use	Colour change
Bromine solution	to test for the presence of carbon-to-carbon double bonds in a molecule	rapidly decolourised
Hot copper(II) oxide	used to oxidise primary and secondary alcohols	black to red
Acidified potassium dichromate (aq)	to oxidise primary and secondary alcohols and aldehydes	orange to green
Tollens' reagent	to oxidise aldehydes	silver mirror formed
Fehling's solution	to oxidise aldehydes	blue to brick red
Benedict's reagent	to distinguish reducing sugars such as glucose and maltose	blue to orange/red
Starch solution	to test for the presence of iodine	blue-black colour formed

THE CHEMISTRY DATA BOOKLET

The data booklet is a valuable source of information and you need to spend time familiarising yourself with the contents. Knowing how to use the book, and being comfortable with using it, will give you invaluable support in the exam. Whilst all the information contained is useful, there are key pages in the data booklet which will really help you.

Page 5 – *the covalent radius*

This gives information on the size of atoms as you cross a period or descend a group.

Page 6 – *the names of the common alkanes, alkenes, alcohols, aldehydes, ketones and carboxylic acids*

– *the formulae of selected oxides and chlorides and their associated melting and boiling points*

These can be used to identify the nature of the bonding in the compound.

Page 7 – *solubilities of selected compounds in water*

– *formulae of selected ions containing more than one type of atom*

These are useful if you're asked to write a chemical formula.

Page 8 – *radioactive decay series*

This will help you in remembering how the mass number and atomic number change when a radioisotope undergoes alpha (α) or beta (β) emission.

Page 10 – *ionisation energies and electronegativities of selected elements*

– You are required to know the definition of ionisation energies, for example 'the first ionisation energy is the energy required to remove one mole of electrons from one mole of gaseous atoms'. If you forget this, then the equations given at the top of this page in the data booklet will help jog your memory.

– The values given in the tables will also help if you are asked to explain a trend across a period or down a group.

Page 11 – *electrochemical series: standard reduction potentials*

- This gives us the ion-electron equations for reduction reactions (gain of electrons) – reading from left to right. For example

$$Fe^{3+} (aq) + e^- \rightarrow Fe^{2+} (aq)$$

- If we reverse the above ion-electron equation then this gives us the oxidation reaction (loss of electrons). For example

$$Fe^{2+} (aq) \rightarrow Fe^{3+} (aq) + e^-$$

- In addition, it provides us with information on the charges associated with most of the common ions and also the formulae for a number of molecules such as iodine (I_2) bromine (Br_2) and chlorine (Cl_2).

Page 12 – *dissociation constants of selected species*

- The information contained in this table is targeted at pupils studying Advanced Higher Chemistry. However, it contains information which can help you:

  i. the formulae of the first four carboxylic acids are given, for example, methanoic acid ($HCOOH$); ethanoic acid (CH_3COOH), and so on

  ii. all the acids given on this page are weak acids, that is, they are only partially ionised when in solution

Page 19 – *values for the commonly used constants*

- If we need to use the Avogadro constant, L, or the Faraday constant, F, or the value for the specific heat capacity of water, then look no further – they are all given on this page.

As said above, a real familiarisation with the data booklet will be an invaluable assistance to you in the preparation for your exam. Take it to your lessons and use it as much as you can when answering questions. The more you use it, the more you will realise how essential it is!

1 Making the Most of Multiple Choice

Unit 1 Energy Matters

Unit 2 World of Carbon

Unit 3 Chemical Reactions

The best way to improve in multiple choice questions is by practice, practice and more practice! There are key questions that seem to come up almost every year and the same pattern is used for other questions. By working through as many examples as you can, you will become familiar with the questions and much more comfortable in answering them.

The multiple choice questions come in very set sections, starting with a few from previous work and then following the pattern of the three Units. They are also a valuable tool in your revision as they can be used to check your understanding and highlight the learning outcomes of the course.

GENERAL ADVICE

Each question follows the same pattern: the stem followed by four answers, one of which you have to pick.

The time allocation for each question is 1 minute 30 seconds, so you should spend no more than 1 hour on this section of the paper. In fact, you will recognise the answer immediately to some of the questions, thereby completing the question in a matter of seconds. This will gain you valuable time to spend on the more demanding questions in other parts of the paper. (However, it is always worth double checking the other answers to make sure you have not leapt to the wrong conclusion.)

A number of questions, essentially the PS type, may require a two-stage operation in order to determine the correct answer and gain the mark. Look at this example.

Example

Solution

Firstly we have to calculate the actual number of moles of HCl used in the reaction. We do this by using the formula:

$$\text{moles} = \text{concentration (mol l}^{-1}) \times \text{volume (litres)}$$

$$= 2 \times 0{\cdot}02$$

$$\text{moles HCl} = 0{\cdot}04$$

Secondly, using the mole ratio – given by the balanced equation – 1 mole Mg reacts with 2 moles HCl. Therefore 0·02 moles Mg will react with 0·04 moles HCl making **B** the correct answer.

On those occasions when you don't immediately recognise the answer, you may be able to eliminate one or two answers. An example of this type of question is as follows.

Example

Solution

You should know that both iodide ion, I^-, and sulphate ion, SO_4^{2-} are negatively charged, therefore answers A and D cannot be correct.

Reduction involves the gain of electrons – it is at this point we can turn to page 11 of the data booklet to help us identify the correct answer.

If we take an example straight from the data booklet we see that when the iron(III) ion is reduced, it gains an electron forming the iron(II) ion:

$$Fe^{3+} + e^- \rightarrow Fe^{2+}$$

Applying the same principle, if cobalt(III) ion gains an electron it will form the cobalt(II) ion: $Co^{3+} + e^- \rightarrow Co^{2+}$. Therefore **C** is the correct answer.

 Always answer every question; do not leave any unattempted. At worst, guess from the answers left after you eliminate any which are obviously wrong.

We will now work through some typical examples putting the above strategies into practice.

UNIT 1 – ENERGY MATTERS

Example

SQA 2008 Section A Q4

A mixture of sodium chloride and sodium sulphate is known to contain 0·6 mol of chloride ions and 0·2 mol of sulphate ions.

How many moles of sodium ions are present?

  A 0·4

  B 0·5

  C 0·8

  D 1·0

Solution

To answer this type of question, we first have to write the correct formula for each compound:

sodium chloride Na^+Cl^- sodium sulphate $(Na^+)_2\ SO_4^{2-}$

Now that we have the correct formulae, which gives us the ratio of ions present, we take each compound in turn to determine the number of moles of sodium ions present.

In sodium chloride the ratio of the chloride ion to sodium ion is 1:1; therefore, if we have 0·6 mol chloride ions then it must also contain **0·6 mol of sodium ions**.

In sodium sulphate the ratio of the sulphate ion to sodium ion is 1:2; therefore, if we have 0·2 moles of sulphate ions then it must contain **0·4 mol of sodium ions**.

Adding together, the number of moles of sodium ions present is 1·0, making answer **D** correct. That is,

Formula	Ion	Ion
Na^+Cl^-	Cl^- 0·6	Na^+ 0·6
$(Na^+)_2\ SO_4^{2-}$	SO_4^{2-} 0·2	Na^+ 0·4

Total number Na^+ ions = 0·6 + 0·4 = 1·0

Example

SQA 2006 Section A Q16

A one-carat diamond used in a ring contained 1×10^{22} carbon atoms.

What is the approximate mass of the diamond?

    A   0·1 g

    B   0·2 g

    C   1·0 g

    D   1·2 g

Solution

A mole of any substance is defined as the Relative Formula Mass expressed in grams. For example, 1 mole of carbon is 12 g. At Higher, you have learned that a mole of a substance contains $6 \cdot 02 \times 10^{23}$ formula units. This number is known as the Avogadro Constant. The formula units can be atoms, molecules or groups of ions.

Therefore: 1 mole of carbon is 12 g and contains $6 \cdot 02 \times 10^{23}$ atoms.

So how do we go about tackling this question?

Taking each answer in turn, calculate the number of moles of carbon first, then multiply by the Avogadro Constant of $6 \cdot 02 \times 10^{23}$ to get the number of carbon atoms present in the diamond ring.

> Remember: moles $= \dfrac{\text{mass}}{\text{formula mass}}$

A moles carbon $= \dfrac{0 \cdot 1 \text{ g}}{12 \text{ g}} = 0 \cdot 008$

→ $0 \cdot 008 \times 6 \cdot 02 \times 10^{23} = 5 \cdot 02 \times 10^{21}$ atoms

B moles carbon $= \dfrac{0 \cdot 2 \text{ g}}{12 \text{ g}} = 0 \cdot 0167$

→ $0 \cdot 0167 \times 6 \cdot 02 \times 10^{23} = 1 \cdot 00 \times 10^{22}$ atoms

Since the number of carbon atoms calculated for **B** matches with the number of atoms (1×10^{22} atoms) given in the stem of the question, it must be the correct answer. However, it is good practice to work out the answers for C and D just to confirm your answer is correct.

C moles carbon $= \dfrac{1 \cdot 0 \text{ g}}{12 \text{ g}} = 0 \cdot 08$

→ $0 \cdot 08 \times 6 \cdot 02 \times 10^{23} = 5 \cdot 02 \times 10^{22}$ atoms

D moles carbon $= \dfrac{1 \cdot 2 \text{ g}}{12 \text{ g}} = 0.10$

→ $0 \cdot 10 \times 6 \cdot 02 \times 10^{23} = 6 \cdot 02 \times 10^{22}$ atoms

Students often find questions involving Avogadro's constant difficult but, with practice, this need not be the case. In fact, these questions all follow a similar pattern.

Example

SQA 2005 Section A Q15

Which of the following gases contains the smallest number of molecules?

    A   100 g fluorine

    B   100 g nitrogen

    C   100 g oxygen

    D   100 g hydrogen

Solution

Remember all the above gases are diatomic. As in the previous example, we will take each answer in turn, calculate the number of moles and then multiply by the Avogadro Constant (6.02×10^{23}).

A moles fluorine = $\dfrac{100\ g}{38\ g} \times 6.02 \times 10^{23} = 1.58 \times 10^{24}$ molecules

B moles nitrogen = $\dfrac{100\ g}{28\ g} \times 6.02 \times 10^{23} = 2.15 \times 10^{24}$ molecules

C moles oxygen = $\dfrac{100\ g}{32\ g} \times 6.02 \times 10^{23} = 1.88 \times 10^{24}$ molecules

D moles hydrogen = $\dfrac{100\ g}{2\ g} \times 6.02 \times 10^{23} = 3.01 \times 10^{25}$ molecules

Comparing all the answers, we see that **A** is the correct answer as it contains the smallest number of molecules.

Example

The equation for the complete combustion of methane is:

$$CH_4(g) + 2O_2(g) \rightarrow CO_2(g) + 2H_2O(l)$$

30 cm³ of methane is mixed with 60 cm³ of oxygen and the mixture is ignited. What is the volume of the resulting gas mixture? (All volumes are measured at the same temperature and pressure.)

    A 30 cm³

    B 60 cm³

    C 90 cm³

    D 120 cm³

Solution

One mole of any (ideal) gas has the same volume as one mole of any other gas under the same conditions of temperature and pressure. This allows us to calculate the volumes of reactant or product involved in a chemical reaction.

A balanced chemical equation gives the relative number of moles of each reactant and product and therefore it also gives the relative volumes.

$CH_4(g)$	+	$2O_2(g)$	$\rightarrow$	$CO_2(g)$	+	$2H_2O(l)$
1 mole		2 moles		1 mole		
1 volume		2 volumes		1 volume		
30 cm³		60 cm³		30 cm³		

|
volume of methane given in the question

From the equation, 30 cm³ of methane gas requires 60 cm³ of oxygen gas to react completely and, on doing so, will produce 30 cm³ of carbon dioxide gas. The volume of the resultant gas is therefore 30 cm³ making **A** the correct answer.

 We have not included the water in the calculation because it is not shown in the equation as a gas. Any reactant or product in the equation which is not a gas is assumed to have zero volume compared to any gas.

Example

We will now look at a similar example but with a slight twist.

SQA 2007 Section A Q16

The equation for the complete combustion of propane is:

$C_3H_8(g) + 5O_2(g) \rightarrow 3CO_2(g) + 4H_2O(l)$

30 cm³ of propane is mixed with 200 cm³ of oxygen and the mixture is ignited. What is the volume of the resulting gas mixture? (All volumes are measured at the same temperature and pressure.)

    A 90 cm³

    B 120 cm³

    C 140 cm³

    D 210 cm³

Solution

We will employ the same method as the previous example.

$$C_3H_8(g) \quad + \quad 5O_2(g) \quad \rightarrow \quad 3CO_2(g) \quad + \quad 4H_2O(\ell)$$

1 mole	5 moles	3 moles
1 volume	5 volumes	3 volumes
30 cm³	150 cm³	90 cm³

|
volume of propane given in the question

Answer A, 90 cm³, would seem the obvious answer but it is incorrect. The correct answer is **C**. Why?

From the equation, 30 cm³ of propane gas requires 150 cm³ of oxygen gas to react completely. However, the question states that 200 cm³ of oxygen was provided. Therefore the resultant gas mixture will also contain 50 cm³ of excess oxygen. This is the slight twist which will catch out many students. The volume of the resultant gas mixture is 90 cm³ of CO_2 + 50 cm³ of excess O_2, giving a total volume of 140 cm³, making **C** the correct answer.

Remember: do not include the water in the calculation as it is not shown as a gas.

Example

SQA 2002 Section A Q9

A metal (melting point 843°C, density 1·54 g cm⁻³) was obtained by electrolysis of its chloride (melting point 772°C, density 2·15 g cm⁻³) at melting point 780°C. During the electrolysis, how would the metal occur?

A   As a solid on the surface of the electrolyte

B   As a liquid on the surface of the electrolyte

C   As a solid at the bottom of the electrolyte

D   As a liquid at the bottom of the electrolyte

Solution

This question tests your ability to use the information given in the question.

If we deal first with the melting point, careful reading of the question informs us that the electrolysis was carried out at 780°C. The melting point of the metal is much higher than this, 843°C, therefore the metal will not have melted and so will occur as a solid. Answers B and D can be eliminated.

We now use the density values. The metal is less dense than the metal chloride; therefore, it will float on the surface. **A** is the correct answer.

Example

> ### SQA 2007 Section A Q11
>
> An element (melting point above 3000°C) forms an oxide which is a gas at room temperature.
>
> Which type of bonding is likely to be present in the element?
>
>   A   Metallic
>
>   B   Polar covalent
>
>   C   Non-polar covalent
>
>   D   Ionic

Solution

This is a tricky PS question. You are given two pieces of information in the stem of the question: the melting point of the element and that the element forms a gaseous oxide at room temperature. This tells us that the oxide has a low boiling point. To start with we can easily eliminate answer D, as ionic bonding only exists in compounds and the question clearly states you are looking for an element.

Now, let's think if the element's melting point can be of value? Yes, it can! The data booklet contains the melting points of all the elements so a quick check (page 4) points us in the direction of carbon as being the element. We should also know that carbon forms oxides which are gaseous at room temperature, that is, CO and CO_2.

We can now rule out A, Metallic, as only metals have metallic bonding. Only non-polar covalent bonds are present in non-metal elements, therefore **C** is the correct answer.

Example

> Proton Nuclear Magnetic Resonance is an analytical technique used to investigate the chemical environment in which the nuclei of the element hydrogen are situated.
>
> From the resultant spectrum the molecular structure can be obtained.
>
> Which of the following molecules would reveal **no** information about its structure?
>
> > A   Fullerene
> >
> > B   Ethanal
> >
> > C   Benzene
> >
> > D   Ethanol

Solution

The question looks difficult, but this is because it is a technique which you are not familiar with. Careful reading of the question is vital, as it tells you the technique will only work if the molecule contains the element *hydrogen*.

Ethanal, benzene and ethanol all contain hydrogen atoms in their structure, so the technique **would** provide information regarding their molecular structure. Fullerene molecules contain no hydrogen atoms, making **A** the correct answer.

 Remember: carbon forms discrete molecules known as fullerenes such as C_{60}, C_{70} and so on.

UNIT 2 – WORLD OF CARBON

You should set aside time and regularly practise the drawing of organic structures. It is time well spent. Use the following examples to test how well you are coping with these questions.

Example

> Butadiene is an early member of a homologous series of hydrocarbons called dienes.
>
> What is the general formula for this series?
>
> > A C_nH_{2n+2}
> >
> > B C_nH_{2n+3}
> >
> > C C_nH_{2n}
> >
> > D C_nH_{2n-2}

Solution

The first step when tackling such a question is to draw the full structural formula for the molecule butadiene. The ending **-diene** tells us that the molecule contains **two** carbon-to-carbon double bonds. The **buta** means it contains **four** carbon atoms.

$$H-\underset{H}{\overset{H}{C}}=C=\underset{H}{\overset{H}{C}}-\underset{H}{\overset{H}{C}}-H$$

number carbon atoms = 4

number of hydrogen atoms = 6

molecular formula = C_4H_6

Now that we know the number of carbon and hydrogen atoms present in the butadiene molecule, we can insert n = 4 into each general formula in turn. A gives C_4H_{10}, B gives C_4H_{11}, C gives C_4H_8 and D gives C_4H_6 which makes **D** the correct answer.

It is always good practice to check your answer. If we take the next member of this homologous series, pentadiene, then its molecular formula, using the general formula C_nH_{2n-2}, should be C_5H_8.

Let's draw its structure and see if we are correct.

$$H-\underset{H}{\overset{H}{C}}=C=\underset{H}{\overset{H}{C}}-\underset{H}{\overset{H}{C}}-\underset{H}{\overset{H}{C}}-H$$

number carbon atoms = 5

number of hydrogen atoms = 8

This fits the general formula.

> The two carbon-to-carbon double bonds do not need to be adjacent to each other.

Example

SQA 2005 Section A Q20

Which of the following organic compounds is an isomer of hexanal?

    A 2-methylbutanal

    B 3-methylpentan-2-one

    C 2,2-dimethylbutan-1-ol

    D 3-ethylpentanal

Solution

This type of question was highlighted by the Principal Assessor as an area of difficulty for candidates. So what is the best approach when tackling this type of question?

Step 1: use the definition of an isomer – **same molecular formula but different structural formula.**

Step 2: draw the structural formula for hexanal:

This allows us to determine its molecular formula: $C_6H_{12}O$.

Step 3: now draw the structural formula for each answer:

Name	Structure	Molecular formula
2-methylbutanal		$C_5H_{10}O$
3-methylpentan-2-one		$C_6H_{12}O$
2,2-dimethylbutan-1-ol		$C_6H_{14}O$
3-ethylpentanal		$C_7H_{14}O$

It is now obvious that **B** is the correct answer because it has the same molecular formula but different structural formula.

Example

Solution

If we first draw the structure of the secondary alcohol and the ketone which would have been produced as a result of the oxidation reaction, and then determine the molecular formulae for each, the answer should be obvious.

```
    H   CH3 H   OH  H
    |    |   |   |   |
H — C — C — C — C — C — H
    |    |   |   |   |
    H    H   H   H   H
      4-methylpentan-2-ol
            C6H14O
```

```
    H   CH3 H   O   H
    |    |   |   ‖   |
H — C — C — C — C — C — H
    |    |   |       |
    H    H   H       H
      4-methylpentan-2-one
            C6H12O
```

The alcohol has lost two hydrogen atoms; thus, the answer is **A**.

It is imperative that you can recognise primary, secondary and tertiary alcohols and what is produced when they are oxidised.

primary alcohol $\xrightarrow{\text{oxidation}}$ aldehyde $\xrightarrow{\text{oxidation}}$ carboxylic acid

secondary alcohol $\xrightarrow{\text{oxidation}}$ ketone

Tertiary alcohols do not undergo oxidation reactions.

Example

SQA 2008 Section A Q22

$$H_3C\!-\!CH\!=\!CH_2$$

Reaction **X** ↓

$$H_3C\!-\!CH_2\!-\!CH_2\!-\!OH$$

Reaction **Y** ↓

$$CH_3\!-\!CH_2\!-\!\underset{\underset{H}{|}}{C}\!=\!O$$

Which line in the table correctly describes reactions **X** and **Y**?

	Reaction X	Reaction Y
A	hydration	oxidation
B	hydration	reduction
C	hydrolysis	oxidation
D	hydrolysis	reduction

Solution

This is a relatively straightforward KU question.

Reaction **X** has converted an alkene into an alcohol. Alkenes undergo addition reactions and in this case we have added water, H_2O. The addition of water is known as hydration. Reaction **X** is hydration. If you are in any doubt about this, note that the product has two hydrogen atoms and one oxygen atom more than the reactant, that is, it has gained the atoms from a water molecule. This allows us to eliminate answers C and D (hydrolysis involves splitting something up), meaning the answer has to be either A or B.

Reaction **Y** has converted an alcohol to an aldehyde. You should know that this is an oxidation reaction. Again, if you are in any doubt about this, note that in an oxidation reaction, the ratio of oxygen to hydrogen atoms increase. That is, in going from the alcohol to the aldehyde, the oxygen:hydrogen ratio has increased from 1:8 to 1:6. The correct answer is therefore **A**.

UNIT 3 – CHEMICAL REACTIONS

Example

SQA 2006 Section A Q37

$HgCl_2(aq) + SnCl_2(aq) \rightarrow Hg(\ell) + SnCl_4(aq)$

Which ion is oxidised in the above redox reaction?

A $Sn^{2+}(aq)$

B $Sn^{4+}(aq)$

C $Hg^{2+}(aq)$

D $Cl^-(aq)$

Solution

The best way to tackle this question is to rewrite the chemical equation in its ionic form where appropriate, ie. only for ionic compunds in solution.

$Hg^{2+}(Cl^-)_2(aq) + Sn^{2+}(Cl^-)_2(aq) \rightarrow Hg(\ell) + Sn^{4+}(Cl^-)_4(aq)$

From this it can be seen that the chloride ion, Cl^-, is a spectator ion – it remains unchanged during, and takes no part in, the reaction. D is incorrect.

At this point we need only concern ourselves with the ions on the left hand side of the ionic equation – these are the ions which are reacting.

Sn^{4+} does not appear on the left hand side of our equation, therefore B must also be incorrect.

Now we turn to the data book and use the Standard Reduction Potentials – **look for the equation on page 11.** The $Hg^{2+}(aq)$ has reacted to form Hg. This is a reduction reaction as it is gaining electrons therefore C is also incorrect.

This leaves **A** as the correct answer. The Sn^{2+} ion is losing electrons (oxidation) to form the Sn^{4+} ion.

$Sn^{2+} \rightarrow Sn^{4+} + 2e^-$

Example

The iodate ion, IO_3^-, can be converted to iodine.

Which is the correct ion-electron equation for this reaction?

A $2IO_3^-(aq) + 12H^+(aq) + 12e^- \rightarrow 2I^-(aq) + 6H_2O(\ell)$

B $IO_3^-(aq) + 6H^+(aq) + 7e^- \rightarrow I^-(aq) + 3H_2O(\ell)$

C $2IO_3^-(aq) + 12H^+(aq) + 11e^- \rightarrow I_2(aq) + 6H_2O(\ell)$

D $2IO_3^-(aq) + 12H^+(aq) + 10e^- \rightarrow I_2(aq) + 6H_2O(\ell)$

Solution

We can immediately eliminate answers A and B – the formula for iodine is I_2.

When asked to write ion-electron equations which are not in the data book then the following method is applied:

- Balance all the elements except hydrogen and oxygen.
- Balance the oxygen by adding water molecules to the side which is short of oxygen.
- Balance the hydrogen by adding hydrogen ions to the side short of hydrogen.
- Balance the charge by adding electrons to ensure that the net charge on the reactants side equals the net charge on the products side.

We can now apply the method.

1 Balance the iodine by multiplying the iodate ion by 2.

$2IO_3^-(aq) \rightarrow I_2(aq)$

2 Balance the oxygen by adding 6 water molecules to the right hand side.

$2IO_3^-(aq) \rightarrow I_2(aq) + 6H_2O(\ell)$

3 Balance the hydrogen by adding 12H^+ ions to the left hand side.

$2IO_3^-(aq) + 12H^+(aq) \rightarrow I_2(aq) + 6H_2O(\ell)$

4 The net charge of the reactants is 10+ and that of the products is 0, so add 10 electrons to the left hand side to balance the charge.

5 $2IO_3^-(aq) + 12H^+(aq) + 10e^- \rightarrow I_2(aq) + 6H_2O(\ell)$

Therefore, **D** is the correct answer.

Example

Solution

This is a relatively easy PS type question requiring you to count the total number of moles of gas on either side of the equation.

A reaction will be unaffected by a change in pressure if the total number of moles of gas on the left hand side equals the total number of moles of gas on the right hand side.

Taking each equation in turn we have:

A	2 moles gas → 1 mole gas	changes in pressure will have an effect
B	2 moles gas → 2 moles gas	changes in pressure will have **no** effect
C	4 moles gas → 2 moles gas	changes in pressure will have an effect
D	3 moles gas → 2 moles gas	changes in pressure will have an effect

Therefore **B** is the correct answer.

In a reaction involving gases, then an increase in pressure moves the equilibrium to the side with a smaller volume – that is, the side with the fewer moles of gas. A decrease in pressure will have the opposite effect.

Example

> **SQA 2008 Section A Q30**
>
> The following equilibrium exists in bromine water.
>
> $$Br_2(aq) + H_2O(\ell) \rightleftharpoons Br^-(aq) + 2H^+(aq) + OBr^-(aq)$$
>
> (red)   (colourless)   (colourless)
>
> The red colour of bromine water would fade on adding a few drops of a concentrated solution of
>
>   A HCl (aq)
>
>   B KBr (aq)
>
>   C AgNO$_3$ (aq)
>
>   D NaOBr (aq)

Solution

The question is asking us to consider the effect of concentration on the position of equilibrium. We can move the equilibrium position to the right by increasing the concentration of the reactants or by removing products.

In A, B and D we are adding **products.** For example, H^+ from HCl, Br^- from KBr and OBr^- from NaOBr all appear on the right hand side of the above equation and as such this will encourage the reverse reaction resulting in the equilibrium position moving to the **left**. We want the equilibrium position to move to the right.

Now that we have eliminated A, B and D to arrive at **C** as the correct answer, it is important to explain why C *is* the correct answer.

If you add Ag^+ ions they will combine with the Br^- ions forming insoluble AgBr(s) (as can be checked in the data book). This effectively removes the Br^- from the right hand side, so the equilibrium position moves to the right, meaning the red colour would fade.

Example

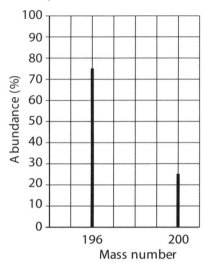
Solution

This is a PS question which requires us to know that when a radioisotope undergoes α-emission the mass number decreases by four, as shown below.

$$^{200}A \rightarrow \ ^{196}B \ + \ ^{4}\alpha$$

From the chart we can now identify that the α-emitting radioisotope has a mass number of 200.

The chart also provides us with the percentage of the α-emitting radioisotope remaining after 8 days: 25%.

We should know that after one half-life 50% of the radioisotope would have remained and after two half-lives 25% would remain. Therefore, the radioisotope has undergone two half-lives in 8 days, meaning the half-life is 4 days, making **B** the correct answer.

Example

SQA 2007 Section A Q39

Strontium-90 is a radioisotope.

What is the neutron:proton ratio in an atom of this isotope?

    A   0·730

    B   1·00

    C   1·37

    D   2·37

Solution

From Standard Grade and Intermediate 2 we should know that

- isotopes are atoms with the same atomic number but different mass number
- the atomic number = number of protons in the nucleus
- number of neutrons = mass number – atomic number

The mass number for the radioisotope strontium is given in the question, i.e. 90. (This is different from the mass number given in the data book but you must use the mass number given in the question.)

Now we use the data book to find the atomic number of strontium, i.e. 38. The number of protons is 38 and the number of neutrons (90 − 38) = 52. We are asked for the neutron to proton ratio so, by setting it out as follows

$$\frac{n}{p} = \frac{52}{38} = 1·37$$

This means **C**, 1·37, is the correct answer.

2 Conquering Calculations

One of the big differences between the Standard Grade or Intermediate 2 courses and the Higher chemistry course is that calculations play a much bigger role. In your S3/S4 course your final exam probably had about 5 or 6 marks allocated to calculations whereas up to 25% of the marks can be gained in calculation questions in Higher. Therefore, calculations are a key area of the course, but they are also an area that can be easily improved with practice.

At first glance, calculations can seem daunting, and all the different types can be confusing. However, nearly all the calculations you will meet in the Higher follow the same pattern; if you can become familiar with a simple step-by-step method then you can tackle almost any question you may be asked. The first thing to remember is that calculations are all about proportion.

Ask yourself the following question: *In a supermarket, 8 apples cost £1.60. How much will 5 apples cost?*

If you get the answer of £1.00, then you have all the tools at your disposal to attempt the Higher calculations. The simple idea of proportion, which you probably do without thinking when shopping, is all that you need. When combined with the methods we will teach you, you will hopefully find calculations become less of a challenge.

IMPORTANT THINGS TO REMEMBER ABOUT CALCULATION QUESTIONS

1   You will need to have a calculator and to be familiar with how to use it. Don't try out a brand new model on the day of your exam!

2   Do not round up your answer. Your final answer should have the same number of significant figures as the numbers in the original question. As a general rule, give your answers to two decimal places.

3   If the question says in bold **show your working clearly**, it means it! While the exam board will give you full marks for an exact correct answer without working, any small mistake will result in no marks at all if working is not shown. If the examiner can follow your train of thought, then you will always get credit for the work that you have done; the examiner marking your paper is trying to give you as many marks as possible!

4   Always give units in your answer. A numerical answer with no units will lose you half a mark, unless the units are included in the question: for example 'calculate the mass, in grams, of magnesium obtained'. However, to ensure you don't miss them when they are important, it is good practice to always give units.

5   Check your answer is reasonable – apply some common sense! Take a minute to look at your final answer, and check that it seems sensible from what you had in the first place and what you know about the experiment. For example, if you started with 3·5 g of an alcohol, you are not going to end up with 564 g of ester. It's likely to be 5·64 g so check your decimal places are in the right place.

 The most important message in all this is that it is vital to show your working. A really silly wrong answer can still end up with most of the credit if most of the steps are right.

CALCULATIONS TYPES IN THE HIGHER EXAM

Here's a list of the main type of calculation you are likely to meet.

Unit 1 – Energy Matters

- calculations of reaction rate from numerical data or graphs (usually graphs)
- calculations involving enthalpies of combustion, enthalpies of solution or enthalpies of neutralisation
- calculations involving the mole and gas volumes
- calculations involving excess reactants

Unit 2 – World of Carbon

- percentage yield calculations (often applied to the PPA on ester formation)

Unit 3 – Chemical Reactions

- Hess's law calculations
- pH calculations
- redox titrations
- calculations based on electrolysis
- radioactivity calculations

We will now look at an example of each kind of calculation and see how we can apply a simple step-by-step method to nearly all questions.

UNIT 1 – ENERGY MATTERS

Calculations of reaction rate from numerical data or graphs

Example

SQA 2005 Section B Q5

The rate of carbon dioxide production was measured when sulphuric acid was added to excess calcium carbonate. The graph obtained is shown.

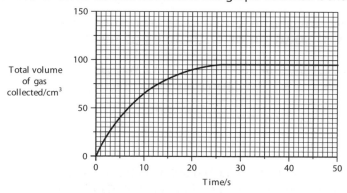

Use the graph to calculate the average reaction rate, in $cm^3\ s^{-1}$, between 10 and 20s.

Solution

This is a fairly standard rate question with the results of the experiment given as a graph.

Calculating the average reaction rate from a graph should not pose too many problems as long as you read the graph carefully and look at the correct section for the information. Also in this question the units are given for you so there is no requirement for you to give them in your answer.

We will use the equation:

$$\text{Rate} = \frac{\text{change in volume (cm}^3)}{\text{change in time (s)}}$$

We read the graph to find out what the volume is at 20 s and at 10 s, and put the numbers into the equation:

$$\text{Rate} = \frac{90 - 65}{20 - 10}$$

$$= \frac{25}{10}$$

$$= 2 \cdot 5 \text{ cm}^3 \text{ s}^{-1}$$

This is a 1 mark question. If you read the graph wrong you would lose a ½ mark.

Calculations involving enthalpies of combustion, enthalpies of solution or enthalpies of neutralisation

The three types of enthalpy question all follow a very similar pattern; this will be the first time we look at a step-by-step breakdown of a calculation.

Enthalpy of combustion

SQA 2002 Section B Q6(c)

In one experiment, the burning of 0·980 g of ethanol resulted in the temperature of 400 cm³ of water rising from 14·2°C to 31·6°C.

Use this information to calculate the enthalpy of combustion of ethanol.

Show your working clearly. (3 marks)

Solution

This is a fairly standard example of an enthalpy of combustion question. The important things to remember here are:

- enthalpies are always related to one mole of a substance
- the unit of all enthalpies is kilojoules per mole, kJ mol^{-1}
- enthalpies of combustion are always exothermic, so ΔH is negative

Let's break the question down.

Step 1: calculate E_h, the heat energy given out or taken in by the water using the equation

$E_h = cm\Delta T$, where

    c = specific heat capacity of water (4·18 kJ kg^{-1} °C^{-1})

    m = mass of water used in experiment, in kg

    ΔT = change in temperature of water, in °C

Therefore, E_h = 4·18 × 0·4 × 17·4

           = 29·09 kJ   **(1 mark)**

To guarantee 1 mark for this step, don't forget to convert the volume of water into kg: volume of water = 400 cm^3 so the mass of water is m = 0·4 kg, and take care when calculating your change in temperature, ΔT (31·6 − 14·2) = 17·4°C.

Step 2: calculate the GFM of the chemical in question

    Ethanol's formula is C_2H_5OH so GFM is 46 g (½)

Step 3: link these two pieces of information together to calculate the ΔH

This is where our idea of proportion comes in. You need to look at the value for Eh and realise that it is the energy produced by burning the mass of ethanol that is given in the question. We want to know how much heat will be generated if we burn 1 mole (46 g) of ethanol.

We can start by stating that 0·980 g of ethanol generates 29·09 kJ of heat energy:

    0·980g ethanol → 29·09 kJ   **(½ mark)**

Now let's think about how much energy would be generated by 1 g (we use 1 g as that can be easily multiplied)

    1g ethanol → $\dfrac{29\cdot09}{0\cdot980}$ kJ

Now we can bring in our GFM

46g ethanol → $\dfrac{46 \times 29\cdot09}{0\cdot980}$ kJ

→ 1365·45 kJ mol^{-1}

Step 4: the enthalpy of combustion of ethanol is **−1365·45 kJ mol^{-1} (1 mark)**

- don't forget the negative sign (you will lose half a mark if you do)
- don't forget the correct units (you will lose another half mark if you do)

Having used this four step method we will now apply it to the other two types of enthalpy question that you need to be able to do.

Enthalpy of solution

As with enthalpy of combustion this enthalpy is always related to one mole of the substance and the units are kJ mol^{-1}. However, there is one key difference. A value for the enthalpy of solution can either be negative or positive:

- ΔH is **negative** when the reaction is exothermic, that is, it involves an increase in temperature
- ΔH is **positive** when the reaction is endothermic, that is, it involves a decrease in temperature

By looking at the temperatures given in the question, or the use of terms such as 'fell' or 'rise', you will need to decide whether your answer will be negative or positive.

Let's look at an example question:

> When 2 g of a substance with a GFM of 60 g is dissolved in 50 cm^3 of water, the temperature fell by 6°C. Calculate the enthalpy of solution of the compound.

Solution

Step 1: heat gained by the water

E_h = cmΔT

= 4·18 × 0·05 ×6

= 1·254 kJ   **(1 mark)**

Step 2: calculate GFM

We don't need to do this step in this question as we have been told it is 60 g.

Step 3: link these two pieces of information together to calculate ΔH

$2g \rightarrow 1{\cdot}254$ kJ

$1g \rightarrow \dfrac{1{\cdot}254}{2}$ kJ

$60g \rightarrow \dfrac{60 \times 1{\cdot}254}{2}$ kJ

$\rightarrow 37{\cdot}6$ kJ mol^{-1}

Step 4: the enthalpy of solution of the compound is **+37·6 kJ mol^{-1}**　　　**(1 mark)**

Remember your units are kJ mol^{-1} (½ mark off for incorrect units)

Because this experiment involved a decrease in temperature, the enthalpy change will be **positive** (an endothermic reaction) (½ mark off for incorrect sign).

It is good practice to show the (+) sign when the reaction is endothermic.

Enthalpy of neutralisation

As before the units are kJ mol^{-1} and the final value is always **negative,** that is, a neutralisation reaction is always exothermic.

Let's work through an enthalpy of neutralisation question:

> 100 cm^3 of 0·8 mol l^{-1} hydrochloric acid at 18°C was added to 100 cm^3 of 0·8 mol l^{-1} sodium hydroxide solution at 18°C. During the reaction, the highest temperature reached by the reaction mixture was 23·5°C.
>
> Calculate the enthalpy of neutralisation for this reaction.　　　**(3 marks)**

Solution

Step 1: you have to assume that the specific heat capacity of a dilute aqueous solution is the same as that of water, and that the total volume of water is the same as the total volume of solution, that is, the volume of acid (100 cm^3) + the volume of alkali (100 cm^3). This allows you to work out the mass, m, to be used.

Total volume of solution = 200 cm^3; therefore the mass, m = 0·20 kg

$\Delta T = (23{\cdot}5 - 18{\cdot}0) = 5{\cdot}5$°C

$E_h = 4{\cdot}18 \times 0{\cdot}20 \times 5{\cdot}5$

$\quad = 4{\cdot}598$ kJ　　　**(1 mark)**

Step 2: this is the step that is slightly different because we need to work out how many moles of water will be formed in the reaction.

First let's look at our balanced equation:

$HCl(aq) + NaOH(aq) \rightarrow NaCl(aq) + H_2O(l)$

1 mole   1 mole   1 mole   1 mole

If we know how many moles of either acid or alkali were used we can use mole ratios to work out the number of moles of water:

number of moles of HCl   = 0·8 mol l^{-1} × 0·1 litres

                           = 0·08 moles

number of moles of NaOH = 0·8 mol l^{-1} × 0·1 litres

                           = 0·08 moles

therefore, number of moles of water formed must be 0·08 moles   **(1 mark)**

Step 3: link these two pieces of information together to calculate ΔH

We know that, in this experiment, 4·598 kJ is produced when 0·08 moles of water are formed, or

0·08 moles water $\rightarrow$ 4·598 kJ

1 mole water $\rightarrow$ $\dfrac{4·598}{0·08}$ kJ

           = 57·48 kJ mol^{-1}

Step 4: the enthalpy of neutralisation is – **57·48 kJ mol^{-1}**   **(1 mark)**

- incorrect units lose ½ mark
- answer not negative loses ½ mark

Calculations involving the mole and gas volumes

Calculations involving gas volumes are pretty straightforward so long as you remember Avogadro's Law: '**one mole of any gas contains the same number of molecules and therefore occupies the same volume (at the same temperature and pressure)**'. Using this law, it follows that the number of moles of a gas is directly proportional to the volume, for example, double the number of moles, double the volume. This means that we can now interchange the number of moles with either the volume of a gas or the mass of a solid. This fact makes these questions remarkably do-able!

Let's look at a past paper question and see how it works:

Example

SQA 2002 Section B Q12

When sodium hydrogencarbonate is heated to 112°C it decomposes and the gas, carbon dioxide, is given off. The equation for the reaction is shown:

$$2NaHCO_3(s) \rightarrow Na_2CO_3(s) + CO_2(g) + H_2O(g)$$

Calculate the theoretical volume of carbon dioxide produced by the complete decomposition of 1·68 g of sodium hydrogencarbonate.

(Take the molar volume of carbon dioxide to be 23 litres mol^{-1}.)

Solution

Step 1: using the balanced equation

We are only interested in the carbon dioxide and the sodium hydrogencarbonate so we can ignore the other chemicals in the equation.

Looking first at our balanced equation we can think about what it tells us regarding the number of moles of sodium hydrogencarbonate and carbon dioxide.

$$2\ NaHCO_3(s) \rightarrow Na_2CO_3(s) + CO_2(g) + H_2O(l)$$

2 moles   1 mole

Step 2: calculate the GFM of the sodium hydrogencarbonate

$NaHCO_3 \rightarrow 23 + 1 + 12 + (3 \times 16) = 84g$ (½ mark)

Step 3: link the pieces of information that you need

Because we are working in numbers of moles, we can use grams (the GFM) for the solid sodium hydrogencarbonate, and litres (the molar volume) for the gaseous carbon dioxide.

2 moles of $NaHCO_3 \rightarrow$ 1 mole of CO_2 (½ mark)

2 × 84g $NaHCO_3 \rightarrow$ 23 litres CO_2 (the molar volume given in the question)

168g $NaHCO_3 \rightarrow$ 23 litres CO_2

$$\text{1g NaHCO}_3 \rightarrow \frac{23}{168} \text{ litres CO}_2$$

$$\text{1·68g NaHCO}_3 \rightarrow \frac{1·68 \times 23}{168} \text{ litres CO}_2$$

$$= \quad 0·23 \text{ litres CO}_2 \qquad \qquad \textbf{(1 mark)}$$

As with other calculations you will lose ½ mark for not giving the correct units.

These questions will often be asked alongside questions involving Avogadro's constant, e.g. 'which volume of gas will contain the most number of particles/molecules/atoms?'

This type of question is covered in the Multiple Choice section of this book.

Calculations involving excess reactants

In your earlier years of studying Chemistry, there was probably an unwritten assumption that there is always an equal balance of reactants and that a reaction will always go to completion using up all the chemicals available. This, in fact, is very rarely true. In most reactions, one reactant will be in excess and will therefore not be completely used up. The reactant that is **not** in excess, that is, the limiting reactant, is the one which will control how much of the product is made. This can be quite a hard concept to grasp so imagine the following scenario:

You are trying to make pairs of one boy and one girl. You have ten boys and eight girls. How many pairs can you make?

Obviously you can only make eight pairs before you 'run out' of girls. That means that the number of pairs you can make is controlled by the girls. Therefore, the girls are the limiting factor and the boys end up being left over and so must be in excess.

Taking this concept back to Chemistry, we can use the balanced chemical equation and the quantities of the reactants provided to calculate which reactant is in excess. Again, we will use a step-by-step process.

Example

A student added 3·27 g of zinc granules to 30 cm³ of 1·0 mol l⁻¹ copper sulphate solution. The balanced equation for the reaction is:

$$\text{Zn(s)} + \text{CuSO}_4\text{(aq)} \rightarrow \text{ZnSO}_4\text{(aq)} + \text{Cu(s)}$$

Show by calculation which reactant is in excess.

Solution

Step 1: using the balanced equation

$Zn(s) + CuSO_4(aq) \rightarrow ZnSO_4(aq) + Cu(s)$

1 mole   1 mole

We need to use the balanced equation to see what the mole ratio of the reactants is. This question is nice and easy as there is a 1 mole: 1 mole ratio.

Step 2: calculate the number of moles of both reactants

- As the zinc is a solid we use the following formulae:

  Zinc moles $= \dfrac{\text{mass}}{\text{RAM}} = \dfrac{3\cdot27\text{ g}}{65\cdot4\text{ g}} = 0\cdot05$

  (½ mark)

- Because the $CuSO_4$ is in solution we use $n = c \times v$.
- Always remember to convert your volume into litres

  $CuSO_4$ moles $= c \times v = 1\cdot0 \times 0\cdot03 = 0\cdot03$ **(½ mark)**

Step 3: taking into account the mole ratio from the balanced equation, make a statement linking these two numbers of moles and conclude which reactant is in excess.

'In the balanced equation there is a ratio of 1 mole:1 mole so 0·05 moles of Zn requires 0·05 moles of $CuSO_4$ to react completely. However, we only have 0·03 moles of $CuSO_4$ available so not all the Zn can react.'

Step 4: → **the Zinc must be in excess**   **(1 mark)**

If the mole ratio is not 1:1 then you must take that into account when deciding how much of one reactant will react with the other. Here is such an example.

Example

Calcium carbonate reacts with hydrochloric acid as follows:

$CaCO_3(s) + 2HCl(aq) \rightarrow CaCl_2(aq) + H_2O(\ell) + CO_2(g)$

4 g of calcium carbonate was added to 50·0 cm³ of 0·20 mol l⁻¹ hydrochloric acid in a beaker.

Show by calculation which reactant is in excess.   **(2 marks)**

Solution

Step 1: using the balanced equation

$$CaCO_3(s) + 2HCl(aq) \rightarrow CaCl_2(aq) + H_2O(\ell) + CO_2(g)$$

1 mole   2 moles

Step 2: calculate the number of moles of both reactants

CaCO$_3$ moles $= \dfrac{\text{mass}}{\text{GFM}} = \dfrac{4\ g}{100\ g} = 0.04$ (½ mark)

HCl moles $= c \times v = 0.2 \times 0.05 = 0.01$ (½ mark)

Step 3: taking into account the mole ratio from the balanced equation, make a statement linking these two numbers of moles and conclude which reactant is in excess.

'In the balanced equation there is a ratio of 1 mole : 2 moles so 0.04 moles of calcium carbonate requires 0.08 moles of HCl to react completely. However, we only have 0.01 moles of HCl available so not all the calcium carbonate can react.'

Step 4: → the calcium carbonate must be in excess   **(1 mark)**

It is very important you show all your working in your calculations as the examiner will be trying to give you as much credit as possible. In excess calculations like these, it is really important that you also explain yourself clearly; you must justify your answer to gain full credit, even for a correct answer.

UNIT 2 – WORLD OF CARBON

Percentage yield calculations

Because this is the only type of calculation covered in Unit 2, it is really common that it comes up in the final exam. However this is not guaranteed!

Another common misconception that you may have had about Chemistry is that all reactions always go through to completion, that is, to give you a 100% yield of product. In reality, this is very unlikely. There are a number of reasons for this, the main one being that many of the reactions are reversible meaning that the conversion of reactants to products is less than 100%.

Obviously, it is important for a chemist to know how much product they are likely to achieve in a particular reaction (in particular in the chemical industry), so this calculation is very important. There are two ways this calculation can be used; we will look at both of them.

Calculating the percentage yield

SQA 2005 Section B Q3b(ii)

Ethanol and ethanoic acid react to form the ester ethyl ethanoate.

| ethanol | + | ethanoic acid | ⇌ | ethyl ethanoate | + | water |

| Mass of 1 mole = 46 g | Mass of 1 mole = 60 g | Mass of 1 mole = 88 g |

Use the above information to calculate the percentage yield of ethyl ethanoate if 5·0 g of ethanol produced 5·8 g of ethyl ethanoate on reaction with excess ethanoic acid.

Solution

Step 1: using the balanced equation

ethanol + ethanoic acid ⇌ ethyl ethanoate + water

1 mole ethanol reacts to give 1 mole of ethyl ethanoate.

As always, the balanced equation is very important. Commonly, these calculations are tied into the PPA on ester formation and so the mole ratio of the reactants and products will be 1:1 – this makes our lives easier!

Step 2: bring in the GFMs of the chemicals and calculate how much product can be made from the mass of the reactant given. Focusing in on the chemicals asked in the question, you first need to calculate the GFMs if you haven't already been given them (which in this case we have).

1 mole ethanol → 1 mole of ethyl ethanoate

46 g ethanol → 88 g ethyl ethanoate

1 g ethanol → $\dfrac{88\ g}{46\ g}$ ethyl ethanoate

$$5.0 \text{ g ethanol} \rightarrow \frac{5.0 \text{ g} \times 88 \text{ g}}{46 \text{ g}} \text{ ethyl ethanoate}$$

$$= 9.57 \text{ g ethyl ethanoate} \qquad \textbf{(1 mark)}$$

This figure of 9·57 g ethyl ethanoate is the **theoretical yield**, that is, the maximum yield that could be obtained if 100% conversion was achieved.

> Notice that we are using the same method of simplifying down to 1 g of the substance that we used in the enthalpy calculations. Hopefully, you will now be able to see how the same basic method can be used to solve all these Higher Chemistry calculations.

Step 3: calculate the percentage yield using the equation

$$\% \text{ yield} = \frac{\text{actual yield}}{\text{theoretical yield}} \times 100$$

(The actual yield is the mass of ester produced, as given in the question.)

Therefore,

$$\% \text{ yield} = \frac{5.8 \text{ g} \times 100}{9.57 \text{ g}} = \textbf{60.6\%}$$

$$\qquad \textbf{(1 mark)}$$

The other way this calculation can be used is to calculate the actual mass of a product that can be made given a percentage yield that has been achieved. The procedure is exactly the same with a simple rearranging of the percentage yield equation in the final step.

Example

SQA 2003 Section B Q6(c)

Starting with a mass of 3·6 g of ethanol, and a slight excess of pentanoic acid, a student achieved a 70% yield of ethyl pentanoate (mass of one mole = 130 g).

Calculate the mass of ester obtained.

Solution

Step 1: on this occasion we are not given an actual equation; however, the mole ratio of the alcohol to ester is always 1:1

1 mole of ethanol reacts to give one mole of ethyl pentanoate

Step 2: bring in the GFMs of the chemicals and calculate the theoretical yield

1 mole ethanol $\rightarrow$ 1 mole ethyl pentanoate

46 g ethanol $\rightarrow$ 130 g ethyl pentanoate

1 g ethanol $\rightarrow$ $\dfrac{130\ g}{46\ g}$ ethyl pentanoate

3·6g ethanol $\rightarrow$ $3·6 \times \dfrac{130\ g}{46g}$ ethyl pentanoate

$\qquad\qquad$ = **10·174 g ethyl pentanoate** $\qquad\qquad$ **(1 mark)**

Step 3: calculate the actual yield by rearranging the % yield equation.

% yield $= \dfrac{\text{actual yield}}{\text{theoretical yield}} \times 100 \rightarrow$ actual yield $= \dfrac{\text{% yield}}{100} \times$ theoretical yield

$\qquad = \dfrac{70}{100} \times 10·174$

$\qquad =$ **7·12 grams** $\qquad\qquad\qquad\qquad\qquad\qquad$ **(1 mark)**

UNIT 3 – CHEMICAL REACTIONS

Hess's Law calculations

Hess's Law allows you to calculate enthalpy changes for reactions which cannot be determined experimentally.

Example

Look at the following equation:

$$C(s) + 2H_2(g) \rightarrow CH_4(g) \qquad \Delta H = ?$$

The enthalpy change, ΔH, for this reaction cannot be determined experimentally, so how do we go about determining it? Well, this is where Hess's Law comes in. The enthalpies of combustion for carbon, hydrogen and methane can be determined experimentally. Using these ΔH values, which are given in the data book, a calculation applying Hess's Law allows us to determine the ΔH for the above reaction.

So how do we go about calculating the ΔH for this reaction? Let's call the equation the 'target equation':

$$\boxed{C(s) + 2H_2(g) \rightarrow CH_4(g)\ \Delta H = ?} \qquad \leftarrow \text{target equation}$$

Solution

Step 1: write **balanced** equations for the combustion of carbon, hydrogen and methane, and write down the values of ΔH for each equation. (You will find these in the data booklet on page 9.) Label them 1, 2 and 3.

		ΔH (kJ mol⁻¹)

$$1 \qquad C(s) + O_2(g) \rightarrow CO_2(g) \qquad\qquad -394$$

$$2 \qquad H_2(g) + \tfrac{1}{2}O_2(g) \rightarrow H_2O(\ell) \qquad\qquad -286$$

$$3 \qquad CH_4(g) + 2O_2(g) \rightarrow CO_2(g) + 2H_2O(\ell) \qquad -891$$

Step 2: this involves rearranging equations 1, 2 and 3 to get the required 'target equation'. The equations may have to be multiplied or reversed in order to achieve this but remember, **whatever you do to the combustion equation you must also do to the value of ΔH:**

- if you have to multiply the equation, you **must multiply the ΔH value**
- if you reverse an equation, you **must reverse the ΔH value,** that is, change the sign

The aim now is to rearrange equations 1, 2 and 3 so that the carbon, hydrogen and methane appear in the same position as they do in the target equation.

Equation 1: carbon is on the left hand side of the equation – this matches its position in the target equation

Equation 2: hydrogen appears on the left hand side of the equation as it does in the target equation. However, we will have to multiply the equation (and ΔH value) by 2 because the target equation has two hydrogens on the left hand side.

Equation 3: methane is on the left hand side of the equation whereas it appears on the right hand side of the target equation. This means the equation will have to be reversed, as will the sign of its ΔH value.

It is easier to rewrite all three equations again at this stage:

		ΔH (kJ mol⁻¹)

$$1 \qquad\qquad C(s) + O_2(g) \rightarrow CO_2(g) \qquad\qquad -394$$

$$2 \times 2 \qquad 2H_2(g) + O_2(g) \rightarrow 2H_2O(\ell) \qquad\qquad \mathbf{-572}\ (-286 \times 2)$$

$$3\ \textbf{reverse}\quad CO_2(g) + 2H_2O(\ell) \rightarrow CH_4(g) + 2O_2(g) \qquad \mathbf{+891}$$

Step 3: now cancel out the water, carbon dioxide and oxygen since similar quantities appear on both sides of the arrows, and add the ΔH values. If we have done it correctly, we should end up with the target equation.

		ΔH (kJ mol^{-1})
1	$C(s) + O_2(g) \rightarrow \cancel{CO_2(g)}$	-394
2 × 2	$2H_2(g) + O_2(g) \rightarrow \cancel{2H_2O(l)}$	-572
3 **reverse**	$\cancel{CO_2(g)} + \cancel{2H_2O(l)} \rightarrow CH_4(g) + \cancel{2O_2(g)}$	$+891$

$$C(s) + 2H_2(g) \rightarrow CH_4(g) \qquad -75$$

$$\Delta H = (-394) + (-572) + (+891)$$

$$= -75 \text{ kJ mol}^{-1.}$$

Let's try one more example – just to make sure we've got it!

Example

SQA 2007 Section B Q12(b)

The equation for the enthalpy of formation of ethyne is:

$$2C(s) + H_2(g) \rightarrow C_2H_2(g)$$

Use the enthalpies of combustion of carbon, hydrogen and ethyne given in the data booklet to calculate the enthalpy of formation of ethyne, in kJ mol^{-1}.

Solution

Target equation → $\boxed{2C(s) + H_2(g) \rightarrow C_2H_2(g)}$

Step 1: write a balanced combustion equation for carbon, hydrogen and ethyne and write down the values of ΔH for each equation:

		ΔH (kJ mol^{-1})
1	$C(s) + O_2(g) \rightarrow CO_2(g)$	-394
2	$H_2(g) + \frac{1}{2}O_2(g) \rightarrow H_2O(l)$	-286
3	$C_2H_2(g) + 2\frac{1}{2}O_2(g) \rightarrow 2CO_2(g) + H_2O(l)$	-1300

Step 2: rearrange equations 1, 2 and 3 so that the carbon, hydrogen and ethyne appear in the same position as they do in the target equation.

● Equation 1 needs to be multiplied by 2, and so must its ΔH value.

● Equation 2 – no changes required.

● Equation 3 needs to be reversed, therefore so must its ΔH value.

		ΔH kJ mol^{-1}
1 × 2	$2C(s) + 2O_2(g) \rightarrow 2CO_2(g)$	−788 (−394 × 2)
2	$H_2(g) + \frac{1}{2}O_2(g) \rightarrow H_2O(\ell)$	−286
3 reverse	$2CO_2(g) + H_2O(\ell) \rightarrow C_2H_2(g) + 2\frac{1}{2}O_2(g)$	+1300

Step 3: now cancel out the water, carbon dioxide and oxygen since similar quantities appear on both sides of the arrows and add the ΔH values.

	ΔH kJ mol^{-1}
$2C(s) + 2\cancel{O_2(g)} \rightarrow 2\cancel{CO_2(g)}$	−788
$H_2(g) + \frac{1}{2}\cancel{O_2(g)} \rightarrow \cancel{H_2O(\ell)}$	−286
$2\cancel{CO_2(g)} + \cancel{H_2O(\ell)} \rightarrow C_2H_2(g) + 2\frac{1}{2}\cancel{O_2(g)}$	+1300
$2C(s) + H_2(g) \rightarrow C_2H_2\ (g)$	+226

$$\Delta H = (-788) + (-286) + (+1300)$$

$$= +226 \text{ kJ mol}^{-1}$$

> It is really important to make sure you show all your working in a question like this. If you do not get the right answer, the examiner will be looking for evidence that you have gone correctly through some of the stages. You will be given credit for each correct combustion equation and its ΔH value (usually ½ mark for each one), and then you will get a further (½ mark) for your final answer. You must show evidence that you have processed at least some of the ΔH values.

pH calculations

These types of questions are pretty straightforward and there is not much variation in the questions that they can ask you. You should also realise that the pH of an aqueous solution is a measure of the concentration of H^+ ions in that solution. The relationship between hydrogen ion concentration and pH is

pH = −(power to which the hydrogen ion concentration is raised)

To calculate the concentration of H^+ ions or OH^- ions in a solution you need to know that the following relationship always holds. (The square brackets are shorthand for concentration in moles per litre.)

$$[H^+] \times [OH^-] = 1 \times 10^{-14}$$

In your notes you will have a table that looks like this:

[H$^+$] mol l^{-1}	pH
1	0
1×10^{-1}	1
1×10^{-2}	2
1×10^{-3}	3
↓	↓
1×10^{-14}	14

You need to be familiar with what this table tells you. For example, what is the pH of a 0·001 mol l^{-1} HCl solution?

$[H^+] = 0·001 = 1 \times 10^{-3}$

Therefore the solution has a pH of 3.

As we have already said, pH questions tend to be quite easy. Let's look at a couple of examples.

Example

A solution has a pH of 4. What is the concentration of H$^+$ ions in this solution?

Solution

Using the previous table, it should be instantly clear that the [H$^+$] will be

1×10^{-4} mol l^{-1}.

Example

A solution has a pH of 10. What is the concentration of OH$^-$ ions in this solution?

Solution

This question is only slightly more complicated! We know from our table that a pH of 10 means that the $[H^+] = 1 \times 10^{-10}$.

We now use the equation

$[H^+] \times [OH^-] = 1 \times 10^{-14}$

So the [OH⁻] must be $\dfrac{1 \times 10^{-14}}{[H^+]} = \dfrac{1 \times 10^{-14}}{1 \times 10^{-10}} = 1 \times 10^{-4}$ mol l⁻¹

Redox titrations

These questions will normally involve you working with ion-electron equations or with a balanced redox equation. It is very important that you are comfortable with using page 11 of the data book and that you know how to construct oxidation and reduction equations for any chemical involved in a reaction. Again, we will work through the calculations in a step-by-step format.

Example

We will start by looking at a question dealing with a balanced redox equation:

> In a titration, a student found that an average of 16·7 cm³ of iron(II) sulphate solution was needed to react completely with 25·0 cm³ of 0·20 mol l⁻¹ potassium permanganate solution.
>
> The equation for the reaction is:
>
> $5Fe^{2+}(aq) + MnO_4^-(aq) + 8H^+(aq) \rightarrow 5Fe^{3+}(aq) + Mn^{2+}(aq) + 4H_2O(\ell)$
>
> Calculate the concentration of the iron(II) sulphate solution, in mol l⁻¹.
>
> **Show your working clearly.**

Solution

Step 1: calculate the number of moles for the reactant about which you have been given information. (Even if all else fails, if you are given the volume and concentration of a solution always use them to work out the number of moles!) In this case, that is the permanganate solution:

No. of moles MnO_4^- = c × v

= 0·2 × 0·025

= 0·005 moles

Step 2: write down the mole ratio of the reactants from the balanced equation:

$MnO_4^-(aq) + 5Fe^{2+}(aq) + 8H^+ \rightarrow 5Fe^{3+}(aq) + Mn^{2+}(aq) + 4H_2O(\ell)$

1 mole   5 moles

So, mole ratio of MnO_4^- : Fe^{2+} = 1:5

Always write the chemical you have used in Step 1 first in the ratio – it will make the rest of the calculation easier.

Step 3: calculate the number of moles for the other reactant using the mole ratio (in this case the Fe^{2+}):

$$\text{number of moles } Fe^{2+} = 5 \times \text{number of moles } MnO_4^-$$
$$= 5 \times 0.005$$
$$= 0.025 \text{ moles}$$

Step 4: now use that number of moles to calculate the concentration:

$$c = \frac{n}{v} = \frac{0.025}{0.0167} = 1.497 \text{ mol l}^{-1} \text{ (or } \mathbf{1.5 \text{ mol l}^{-1}}\text{)}$$

Always remember to convert all your volumes into litres.
Take care to give the correct final units.

A redox titration calculation can be directly linked to the PPA on the determination of the mass of vitamin C in a tablet. Such questions occur quite often.

Example

Let's now look at a calculation based on the vitamin C PPA.

> A standard solution of iodine can be used to determine the mass of vitamin C in a tablet. The equation for the reaction is:
>
> $$C_6H_8O_6(aq) + I_2(aq) \rightarrow C_6H_6O_6(aq) + 2H^+(aq) + 2I^-(aq)$$
>
> A vitamin C tablet was dissolved in some water and the solution was made up to 250 cm³. 25 cm³ portions of this solution were found to react completely with an average of 27·2 cm³ of 0·021 mol l⁻¹ iodine solution.
>
> Calculate the mass of vitamin C present in the tablet.

55

Solution

Step 1: calculate the number of moles for the reactant about which you have been given information. In this case, it's the iodine solution.

$$\text{moles } I_2 = c \times v$$
$$= 0.021 \times 0.0272$$
$$= 0.0005712 \text{ moles}$$

Step 2: write down the mole ratio of the reactants from the balanced equation:

$$C_6H_8O_6 + I_2 \rightarrow C_6H_6O_6 + 2H^+ + 2I^-$$

  1 mole   1 mole

Nice and easy – a 1:1 ratio

Step 3: calculate the number of moles for the other reactant using the mole ratio.

As the ratio is 1:1, the number of moles of $C_6H_8O_6$ will also be 0.0005712 moles.

Step 4: multiply this number of moles to obtain the number of moles for the whole 250 cm³ sample.

> This is the step most pupils forget to do! Remember that the number of moles you have just calculated refers only to a 25 cm³ sample and you need to know how many moles were present in the whole tablet which was dissolved in a 250 cm³ solution.

To go from 25 cm³ to 250 cm³ we need to multiply by 10, so:

  total number of moles of vitamin C is $10 \times 0.0005712 = 0.005712$ moles

Step 5: find the mass of vitamin C present in the tablet

To do this, we first need to calculate the mass of 1 mole of vitamin C:

  $C_6H_8O_6$ one mole will weigh $(6 \times 12) + (8 \times 1) + (6 \times 16) = 176$ g

The mass of the vitamin C in the tablet is therefore

  number of moles × GFM $= 0.005712 \times 176$
  $= 1.0053$ g

> As with all our calculations, we should now look at this answer and check that it is reasonable. As a vitamin C tablet will be around 1 g in weight, this is a sensible answer. It is good practice to always check your answers in this way.

Calculations based on electrolysis

Electrolysis calculations nearly always follow the same set of routines. When we electrolyse a substance, electricity is passed through it and it decomposes into its elements. How much product you get depends on how much electricity you pass through the circuit.

The important thing to know in these calculations is that the quantity of electricity, the **charge** (Q) is measured in **coulombs** (C) and can be calculated using the equation:

$$\text{charge (Q)} = \text{current (I)} \times \text{time (t)}$$

$$\underset{\text{coulombs}}{|} \qquad \underset{\text{amps}}{|} \qquad \underset{\text{seconds}}{|}$$

We then use the number known as Faraday's constant to calculate the number of moles of electrons which have passed through the substance. Faraday's constant is 96 500 C. This means that each time 1 mole of electrons is transferred through the circuit, 96 500 C are involved. If we know how many electrons are involved in the ion-electron equation for the chemical in question, then we can work out how many moles of product have been formed.

 It is vital that you **always** convert your time into seconds.

These questions tend to follow a fairly standard pattern. Let's try a couple.

Example

SQA 2006 Section B Q15

Chlorine can be produced commercially from concentrated sodium chloride solution in a membrane cell.

Only sodium ions can pass through the membrane. These ions move in the direction shown in the diagram.

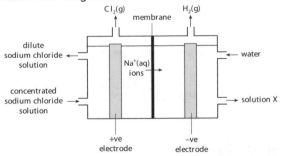

The reactions at each electrode are:

+ve electrode: $2Cl^-(aq) \rightarrow Cl_2(g) + 2e^-$

−ve electrode: $2H_2O(l) + 2e^- \rightarrow H_2(g) + 2OH^-(aq)$

Calculate the mass of chlorine, in kilograms, produced in a membrane cell using a current of 80 000 A for 10 hours.

Show your working clearly.

Solution

Step 1: calculate the charge

$Q = I \times t$

$= 80\ 000 \times (10 \times 60 \times 60)$ (remember to convert time into seconds)

$= 2{\cdot}88 \times 10^9$ C   **(1 mark)**

Step 2: write down the ion-electron equation for the chemical you have been asked about and, using Faraday's constant, calculate the number of coulombs required to obtain 1 mole of the substance.

Chlorine: $2Cl^- \rightarrow Cl_2 + 2e^-$

2 electrons in equation so multiply Faraday's constant by 2:

$2 \times 96\ 500 = 193\ 000$ C

Therefore the number of coulombs required to generate 1 mole of chlorine is 193 000 C   **(1 mark)**

Step 3: calculate the mass of chlorine obtained

1 mole of chlorine (Cl_2) has a mass of 71 grams

So, 193 000 C are required to generate 71 grams of chlorine

$1C \rightarrow \dfrac{71}{193\ 000}$ grams of chlorine

But, we have $2{\cdot}88 \times 10^9$ C generated in this experiment so:

2.88×10^9 C $\rightarrow 2{\cdot}88 \times 10^9 \times \dfrac{71}{193\ 000}$ grams of chlorine

$= 1059481{\cdot}9$ grams of chlorine

$= \mathbf{1059{\cdot}50}$ **kg of chlorine**   **(1 mark)**

Take special care with this type of question. You were asked to give your answer in kilograms – don't forget to do so!

Example

Let's try a slightly different question:

SQA 2003 Section B Q16

A student electrolysed dilute sulphuric acid using the apparatus shown in order to estimate the volume of one mole of hydrogen gas.

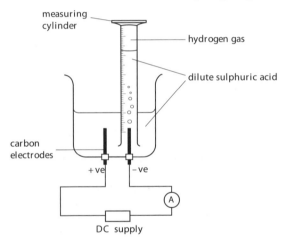

The measurements recorded by the student were:

Current = 0·5 A

Time = 14 minutes

Volume of hydrogen collected = 52 cm³

Calculate the molar volume of hydrogen gas.

Show your working clearly.

This question is slightly different because it is asking to calculate a molar volume. (Remember that is the volume occupied by 1 mole of a gas.) However, in the main, we will answer it using the same method.

Solution

Step 1: calculate the charge in the circuit

$$Q = I \times t$$
$$= 0 \cdot 5 \times (14 \times 60)$$
$$= 420 \text{ C}$$
(1 mark)

Step 2: write down the ion-electron equation for the chemical you have been asked about and, using Faraday's constant, calculate the number of coulombs required to obtain 1 mole of the substance

$$2H^+ + 2e^- \rightarrow H_2$$

There are 2 electrons in the equation so multiply Faraday's constant by 2:

$$2 \times 96\ 500 = 193\ 000 \text{ C}$$

Therefore the number of coulombs required to generate 1 mole of hydrogen is 193 000 C
(1 mark)

Step 3: calculate the molar volume of the hydrogen gas

In the question we were told that 52 cm³ of hydrogen gas was collected, and we know that this experiment generated 420 C of charge.

Put another way 420 C produced 52 cm³ of hydrogen (0·052 litres).

We need to know what volume would be produced if 193 000 C were used as that is the charge required to produce 1 mole of hydrogen. Using the same method we have now used several times:

$$420 \text{ C} \quad \rightarrow \quad 0 \cdot 052 \text{ litres hydrogen}$$

$$1 \text{ C} \quad \rightarrow \quad \frac{0 \cdot 052}{420} \text{ litres of hydrogen}$$

$$193\ 000 \text{ C} \rightarrow 193\ 000 \times \frac{0 \cdot 052}{420} \text{ litres of hydrogen}$$

$$= 23 \cdot 9 \text{ litres of hydrogen}$$

That is, the molar volume of hydrogen is **23·9 litres**
(1 mark)

> Check again – is this reasonable? At room temperature molar volumes are about 24 litres so, yes, this is a reasonable answer.

> Quantitative electrolysis calculations will be worth either 2 or 3 marks. For a 2 mark question you will be given the ion-electron equation required, but for a 3 mark question you are expected to write the appropriate ion-electron equation yourself. It is worth practising how to do this. However you can always use your data booklet page 11 to help you.

Radioactivity calculations

There are very few calculations based on radioactivity. The two main types are writing balanced nuclear decay equations (which involve simple arithmetic) and half-life calculations. Let's look at a balanced decay equation first.

Example

> Write a balanced nuclear equation for the alpha decay of uranium-238.

Solution

You should know that alpha decay involves the mass number decreasing by 4 and the atomic number decreasing by 2. Bearing in mind that the mass number goes at the top left and the atomic number goes at the bottom left, your answer should look like this:

$$^{238}_{92}U \rightarrow \ ^{234}_{90}Th + ^{4}_{2}He$$

The product of decay (in this case the alpha particle) is always on the right hand side of the equation. This is a 1 or 0 question.

The other kind of radioactivity calculation you may meet involves half-life. You should know that the half-life is the time taken for the radioactivity of a sample to fall by 50%.

Half-life questions are a case of simple arithmetic and, quite often, just being able to count!

Example

The half-life of phosphorus-32 is 14·3 days.

Calculate the time it would take for the mass of phosphorus-32 in an 8 g sample to fall to 1 g.

Solution

The mass will fall by half with each half-life as the whole sample is radioactive:

$8\,g \rightarrow 4\,g \rightarrow 2\,g \rightarrow 1\,g$

Therefore there are 3 half-lives.

$3 \times 14{\cdot}3$ days = **42·9 days**   (½ **for number of half-lives**

½ **for the answer)**

Final advice

To reiterate what we said at the beginning of this chapter, the key to success at calculations is to practise as many examples as you can. Using the methods from this book will help you to logically and methodically optimise your chances of gaining the most marks possible.

3 Tidying up Trends in the Periodic Table

Although this is not the biggest section of work, questions on the Periodic Table are a regular feature in the final exam. Questions relating to the trends in properties of elements across a period or down a group are often poorly answered.

It would be fair to say that almost all the properties of the elements rely on the attraction between the outer electrons and the nucleus. In general, the trends in the properties of elements usually depend on the following factors:

- the nuclear charge, that is, the number of protons in the nucleus
- the number of the energy level or shell occupied by the outer electrons
- the screening of the outer electron from the attraction of the nucleus by the inner shell electrons

One or more of the above factors will determine whether the attraction of the nucleus for the outer electrons increases or decreases as we go across a period or descend a group. The following is a quick reminder.

Li   Be   B   C   N   O   F   Ne

Na

atomic size decreases →
ionisation energy increases→

K

Why?
– nuclear charge increases
– electrons occupy the same energy level

Rb

so electrons more strongly held

Cs

↓   atomic size increases
ionisation energy decreases

Why?
– outer electron is in an energy level
  further away from the nucleus
– complete inner shells screen the outer
  electron from nuclear attraction

**so electrons are further from the nucleus
and less strongly held**

EXAMPLE QUESTIONS

Example

> **SQA 2000 Section A Q8**
>
> The difference between the atomic size of sodium and chlorine is mainly due to the differences in the
>
> A   number of electrons
>
> B   number of protons
>
> C   number of neutrons
>
> D   mass of each atom.

Solution

If we refer to the data booklet we see that the elements sodium and chlorine are in the same period of the Periodic Table. The atomic size decreases across a period from left to right as a result of the increasing nuclear charge. The nuclear charge is related to the number of protons in the nucleus, therefore answer **B** is correct.

Example

> **SQA 2007 Section B Q1(b)**
>
> Atoms of different elements are different sizes.
>
> What is the trend in atomic size across the period from sodium to argon?

Solution

We are simply being asked to state whether the atomic size increases or decreases as we go across the period. The covalent radius of each element is taken as a measure of the size of an atom. If we turn to page 5 of the data booklet, we can clearly see that the atomic size decreases across the period from sodium to argon. The simple answer **'decreases'** would get the mark.

Example

> **SQA 2006 Section B Q2(a)**
>
> Why does the atomic size decrease crossing the period from lithium to neon?

Solution

Across the period, the nuclear charge increases, while the outer electrons all occupy the same energy level. The increase in nuclear charge means the outer electrons are pulled closer to the nucleus, resulting in a decrease in the atomic size.

Example

> **SQA 2007 Section B Q1(c)**
>
> Atoms of different elements have different ionisation energies.
>
> **Explain clearly** why the first ionisation energy of potassium
> is less than the first ionisation energy of sodium.　　　　　**(2 marks)**

Solution

 The first ionisation energy of an element is the energy required to remove one mole of electrons from one mole of gaseous atoms.

If we pause for a minute and think about the definition of the ionisation energy, then it should be clear that the further away the outer electron is from the nucleus the less energy will be required to remove it.

It is extremely helpful when answering questions of this type to write down the electron arrangement for each element. These can be found on page 2 of the data booklet:

　　Na atom = 2,8,1

　　K atom　= 2,8,8,1

Using the electron arrangements we clearly see that, in the case of potassium, **the outer electron is in an energy level further away from the nucleus.**

(1 mark)

In addition, there will be a **greater screening effect due to more shells of inner electrons**.

(1 mark)

Both of these reasons account for the first ionisation energy of potassium being less than that of sodium, and both are required to gain the two marks.

Example

The graph shows the first three ionisation energies for magnesium.

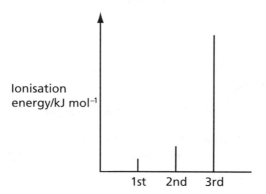

Ionisation
energy/kJ mol^{-1}

1st   2nd   3rd

Why is the third ionisation energy of magnesium so much higher than the second ionisation energy?

(1 mark)

Solution

Because the electron arrangement for the magnesium atom is 2,8,2 the first two electrons are removed from an incomplete shell. This leaves the electron arrangement for the Mg^{2+} ion as 2,8. Therefore, the third electron would have to be removed from this full (or complete) shell. This is a very stable arrangement and requires a lot more energy to be disrupted.

 A similar jump in energy will occur whenever the removal of an electron from a full shell is attempted, for example, removing the second electron from lithium or the fourth electron from aluminium.

Example

SQA 2004 Section A Q9

Which of the following elements has the greatest electronegativity?

    A Caesium

    B Oxygen

    C Fluorine

    D Iodine

Solution

To answer this question we turn to page 10 of the data booklet and find the element with the greatest electronegativity. It is just a case of comparing the values given in the table – the larger the value the greater the electronegativity.

Caesium = 0·8   Oxygen = 3·5   Fluorine = 4·0   Iodine = 2·6

So the answer is **C**, fluorine.

Becoming Better at Bonding

The area of bonding is one that students find most demanding. However, on closer inspection, you should see that much of the theory has been covered already in S3 and S4. We are now going to give you an overview of this very important topic, and then look at how you can maximise the numbers of marks when answering the questions.

Firstly, here is a quick recap of what you should know.

Elements			
Metals			
Example	**Bonding**	**Structure**	**Properties**
Na, Cu, Sn	metallic	lattice	Conduct electricity when solid or liquid.
Non-metals			
Example	**Bonding**	**Structure**	**Properties**
C, Si, B	covalent	network	Do **not** conduct electricity in any state. Have very high melting points.
			Diamond
O_2, N_2, S	covalent	molecular	Do **not** conduct electricity in any state. Low melting and boiling points.
			$N\equiv N$ S_8 Crown
He, Ne, Ar	–	monatomic	Very low melting and boiling points.

Compounds			

Ionic

Examples	Bonding	Structure	Properties
Na^+Cl^- $(K^+)_2O^{2-}$ $Ca^{2+}SO_4^{2-}$	ionic	lattice	Conduct electricity when molten or in solution. Solid at room temperature. Tend to have high melting points. Some soluble in water (always refer to data book).

Na^+Cl^- lattice

Covalent

A. Many covalent compounds exist as discrete molecules. The atoms within the molecule are covalently bonded to each other.

Examples	Bonding	Structure	Properties
CO_2, CH_4 NH_3, H_2O $C_6H_{12}O_6$	covalent	molecular	Do **not** conduct electricity in any state. Usually liquids or gases at room temperature.

CH_4

$O=C=O$

CO_2

B. Some covalent compounds have a covalent network structure. The atoms are covalently bonded within the network structure.

Examples	Bonding	Structure	Properties
SiO_2, SiC	covalent	network	Do **not** conduct electricity in any state. Have very high melting points. Unreactive. Insoluble in water.

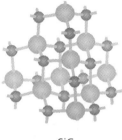

SiC

EXAMPLE QUESTIONS

Now let's look at a few questions from past papers.

Example

SQA 2008 Section B Q1

The formulae for three oxides of sodium, carbon and silicon are Na_2O, CO_2 and SiO_2.

Complete the table for CO_2 and SiO_2 to show both the bonding and structure of the three oxides at room temperature.

Oxide	Bonding and structure
Na_2O	ionic lattice
CO_2	
SiO_2	

(2 marks)

Solution

This is a very straightforward question. You are expected to know that silicon dioxide, SiO_2, is a **covalent network** structure (½ for covalent and ½ for network). Carbon dioxide, CO_2, exists as a **covalent molecule** (½ for covalent and ½ for molecule).

Example

Tin(IV) chloride is a colourless liquid with a boiling point of 114°C.

Name the type of bonding in tin(IV) chloride.   **(1 mark)**

Solution

The unwary candidate will answer 'ionic', since the compound contains a metal and a non-metal. This is incorrect.

You should never assume that the combination of a metal and a non-metal means that the bonding is ionic. Ionic compounds are always solid at room temperature and have high melting and boiling points due to the strong attractions between the oppositely charged ions. From the information given in the question, tin(IV) chloride has none of these properties. In fact, it is a liquid at room temperature and has a low boiling point. Therefore the bonding must be **covalent**.

When deciding on the type of bonding, you can use the following as a guide, but remember it is nothing more than that.

● As a general rule, the further apart the elements are in the Periodic Table the more likely the bonding will be ionic (i.e. KCl, LiCl).

● We can use the electronegativity values for each element in the compound and calculate the difference:

   ○ atoms with similar or identical electronegativities form non-polar covalent bonds (for example, PH_3)

   ○ atoms with noticeably different electronegativities form polar covalent bonds (for example, HCl)

   ○ a large difference in electronegativity would tend to suggest the bonding is ionic. For example, Cs = 0·8, F = 4·0, difference = 3·2 therefore ionic

Example

The two hydrogen atoms in a molecule of hydrogen are held together by

   A a hydrogen bond

   B a polar covalent bond

   C a non-polar covalent bond

   D a van der Waals' force

Solution

The question is asking us to consider the nature of the **intra**molecular bond, that is, the bond **within** the molecule. Therefore answers A and D can be eliminated immediately as these are forces of attraction **between** molecules.

Next we can use the electronegativitity values from page 10 of the data booklet to make decisions with respect to the type of bond holding the atoms together. Since the question is related to the hydrogen molecule, H_2, the atoms have identical electronegativities. Therefore **C** must be the correct answer.

Example

The melting and boiling points and electrical conductivities of three substances are given in the table.

Substance	Melting point (°C)	Boiling point (°C)	Solid conducts electricity?	Melt conducts electricity?
A	92	190	no	no
B	773	1407	no	yes
C	883	2503	no	no

Identify the type of bonding and structure in each substance.

Solution

This question is very much based on Standard Grade and Intermediate 2 work.

Ionic compounds only conduct electricity when molten or in solution. Therefore substance B must have ionic bonding and a lattice structure.

Covalent compounds do not conduct electricity in any state so A and C are covalent. Substance C has a high melting and boiling point, therefore it must have a covalent network structure.

A has covalent molecules.

INTERMOLECULAR FORCES

Questions relating to intermolecular forces of attraction are often highlighted as being poorly answered by candidates. The questions usually ask you to identify the forces of attraction between molecules or to explain the difference between the melting or boiling points of two molecules with similar molecular masses.

Here is a quick reminder:

- **Van de Waals' forces** are a result of the electrostatic attraction between temporary dipoles caused by the movement of electrons in atoms and molecules. They are the only force of attraction between non-polar molecules such as H_2, N_2, O_2, CH_4 and C_2H_6 and are considered to be weak, but this is only in comparison to the other intermolecular forces of attraction between molecules of similar molecular mass.

  Permanent dipole–permanent dipole attractions are the electrostatic force of attraction between polar molecules (the molecule is polar due to it having a permanent dipole). In molecules such as HCl, the chlorine atom is more electronegative than the hydrogen atom and, as a result, the chlorine atom is always slightly negative and the hydrogen atom is always slightly positive. As a result of this, the slightly positive hydrogen atom of one molecule will be attracted to the slightly negative chlorine atom of another molecule.

  $$^{\delta+}H - Cl^{\delta-} \ \text{\tiny IIII} \ ^{\delta+}H - Cl^{\delta-} \ \text{\tiny IIII} \ ^{\delta+}H - Cl^{\delta-}$$

  They are stronger than van der Waals' forces for molecules of similar molecular mass.

- **Hydrogen bonding**

  Bonds consisting of a hydrogen atom bonded to an atom of a highly electronegative element such as nitrogen, oxygen or fluorine are polar. The electrostatic force of attraction between molecules which contain these polar bonds is known as **hydrogen bonding**. In molecules such as water, H_2O, the oxygen atom is much more electronegative than the hydrogen atom, so the oxygen atom is always slightly negative and the hydrogen atom is always slightly positive. The slightly positive hydrogen atom in one water molecule will be attracted to the slightly negative oxygen atom in another water molecule.

These are the strongest type of intermolecular force between molecules of similar molecular mass.

Remember, as mentioned above, that hydrogen bonding only occurs between molecules which contain either H—N, H—O or H—F.

Melting and boiling points are a reflection of the force of attraction between molecules.

We will now consider a few questions and how we should go about answering them.

Example

SQA 2001 Section A Q10

Which type of bonding can be described as intermolecular?

A Covalent bonding

B Hydrogen bonding

C Ionic bonding

D Metallic bonding

Solution

This is a simple KU question which requires you to be aware that the term **inter** means **between** molecules.

We can rule out answer A because covalent bonds are **intra**molecular, that is, they are found **within** the molecule. Ionic bonding is the electrostatic force of attraction between positive and negative ions, while only metals have metallic bonding, so answers C and D must be wrong.

Therefore the correct answer is **B**, hydrogen bonding.

Example

SQA 2002 Section A Q8

The shapes of some common molecules are shown below and each contains at least one polar covalent bond.

Which molecule is non-polar?

A   H—F

B   O=C=O

C   H $\diagup$ O $\diagdown$ H

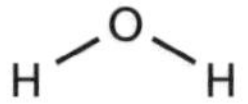

D   H $\diagup$ N $\diagdown$ H
            |
            H

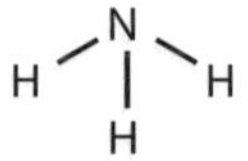

Solution

The question is asking you to consider the symmetry of molecules. All four molecules contain polar covalent bonds; however, if the molecule is completely symmetrical then the polarity of the bonds cancel out and overall the molecule is non-polar.

You are expected to know that CO_2 is highly symmetrical and, as a result, its molecules are non-polar. The correct answer is **B**.

Example

H   H
| |
H—C—C—H   H—C===O
| | |
H   H   H

ethane   methanal
molecular mass 30   molecular mass 30
boiling point −89°C boiling point −21°C

Methanal and ethane have identical molecular masses, but methanal has a much higher boiling point.

In terms of the intermolecular bonding present, **explain** why methanal has a much higher boiling point than ethane.   **(2 marks)**

Solution

Notice that this question carries 2 marks and, in this instance, the mark scheme will be based on (4 × ½). Therefore we are looking for four distinct points in our answer.

Because the two compounds have identical molecular masses, it is important to recognise that the difference in boiling points is a reflection of the strength of the intermolecular forces between them. Your answer should make the connection between the strength of the force and the difference in boiling point.

In methanal, the carbon and oxygen atoms have different electronegativity values. Carbon is 2·5 and oxygen is 3·5, and this results in the $^{\delta+}C{=}O^{\delta-}$ bond being polar, with the carbon atom carrying a slight positive charge (δ^+) and the oxygen atom being slightly negative because the oxygen (δ^-) has the greater attraction for the shared electrons. Because the molecule is not symmetrical, it has a permanent dipole and is therefore a polar molecule.

Now we have to decide whether the intermolecular force of attraction between the molecules is caused by permanent dipole–permanent dipole attractions or by hydrogen bonds.

It is clear from the structure of methanal that no hydrogen atoms are bonded to a highly electronegative nitrogen, oxygen or fluorine atom; thus we can immediately rule out hydrogen bonds. Therefore, methanal has permanent dipole–permanent dipole attractions between its molecules. Ethane is a non-polar molecule with van der Waals' forces between its molecules.

A full answer here should state the following.

- Methanal has permanent dipole–permanent dipole attractions between its molecules. (½ **mark**)

- Ethane, however, being a non-polar molecule (it has no permanent dipole) has only **van der Waals' forces** between its molecules. (½ **mark**)

- Permanent dipole–permanent dipole attractions are **stronger** than van der Waals' forces. (½ **mark**)

- **Therefore, more energy is required** to overcome them, resulting in methanal having a higher boiling point. (½ **mark**)

Example

SQA 2008 Section B Q15 part (b)

Boiling points can be used to compare the strengths of intermolecular forces in alkanes with the strengths of the intermolecular forces in diols.

Name the alkane that should be used to make a valid comparison between the strength of its intermolecular forces and those in ethane-1,2-diol.

Solution

To answer this question we have to know that, in order to make a valid comparison of the strength of the intermolecular forces of attraction between molecules, the alkane **must have an identical or very similar molecular mass to that of ethane-1,2-diol.**

The best approach is to draw out the structure of the diol in order to determine its molecular mass.

ethane-1,2-diol
molecular mass = 62

The alkane with a similar molecular mass to that of the diol is **butane**, C_4H_{10}, which has a molecular mass of 58.

Example

Solution

To answer this question we first have to identify the intermolecular force of attraction present in ammonia.

Ammonia has hydrogen atoms bonded to the highly electronegative element nitrogen. The presence of these bonds will lead to **hydrogen bonding** occurring between molecules of ammonia. **(½ mark)**

Hydrogen bonds are the **strongest of the intermolecular forces,** and this is why ammonia has a relatively high boiling point compared to other molecules of similar molecular mass. **(½ mark)**

These two points make up the first mark.

> Because the question is worth 2 marks, a fuller explanation is required than to simply state that the relatively high boiling point is due to hydrogen bonding. At Higher level you have to work a bit harder to get full marks.

To obtain the second mark you have to go a bit deeper and explain the origins of hydrogen bonding. In essence, you have to mention the difference in electronegativity values between nitrogen and hydrogen which results in the N—H bonds being highly polar.

Your answer should be as follows.

In ammonia, the nitrogen and hydrogen atoms have different electronegativity values. Nitrogen is 3·0 and hydrogen is 2·2, and this results in the nitrogen atom always carrying a slightly negative charge (δ^-), and the hydrogen atom always being slightly positive (δ^+). This means that the $^{\delta-}$N—H$^{\delta+}$ bond is highly polar. **(1 mark)**

Example

Adhesive plastic strips containing hydrogen peroxide, H_2O_2, in a gel can be used to whiten teeth. In the gel, molecules of hydrogen peroxide and urea are held together as shown.

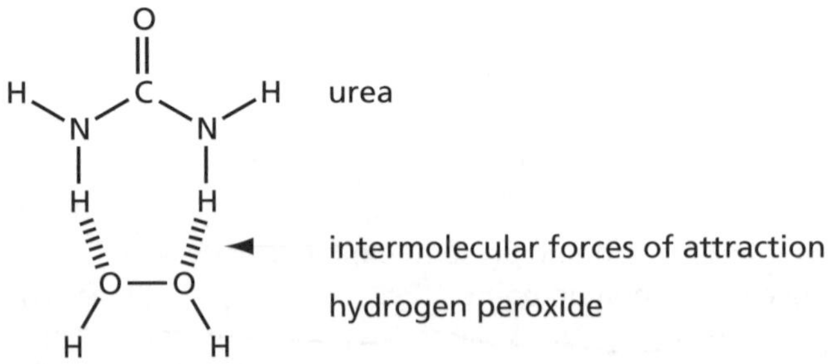

urea

intermolecular forces of attraction

hydrogen peroxide

Name the type of intermolecular force that is responsible for holding these molecules of hydrogen peroxide and urea together. **(1 mark)**

Solution

We are being asked to name the intermolecular force of attraction, meaning that we have to decide if it is van der Waals', permanent dipole–permanent dipole or hydrogen bonding.

On inspecting the above diagram, we see that both the urea and hydrogen peroxide molecules have hydrogen atoms attached directly to the highly electronegative atoms: nitrogen (in the case of urea), and oxygen (in the hydrogen peroxide). As a result both molecules contain highly polar bonds. Therefore, **hydrogen bonds** will form between the hydrogen atoms in the urea molecule and the oxygen atoms in the hydrogen peroxide molecule.

Notice the question leads you to give a one word answer by asking 'Name', so a full explanation of why the answer is hydrogen bonds is not required to gain the mark.

Example

> **SQA 2009 Section B Q1(c)**
>
> The graph shows the boiling points of elements in Group 7 of the Periodic Table.
>
>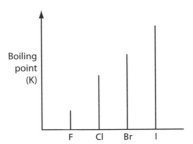
>
> Why do boiling points increase down Group 7?

Solution

Although the question carries only one mark, a response such as 'more energy is needed' or 'the molecular size is increasing', would not be enough to gain the full mark. In addition, when answering a question like this, it is best to avoid vague terms like 'size'.

The full mark is made up of (2 x ½) so you need to give an answer such as: 'As the molecular mass **increases**, the **strength of the van der Waals' forces between** the molecules **increases**.'

Example

> Nitrogen trichloride, NCl_3, has a boiling point of 71°C.
>
> Name the intermolecular force of attraction that has to be overcome when nitrogen trichloride vapourises. **(1 mark)**

Solution

To answer this question we use the electronegativity values given in the data booklet. Nitrogen has a value of 3·0 and chlorine also has a value of 3·0. Since the values are identical, the molecule will have no permanent dipole and so the intermolecular force of attraction will be **van der Waals'**.

SOLUBILITY

If asked to explain the solubility, or lack of it, of two compounds (for example, 'why is ethanol soluble in water?'), you should remember the following rules:

- **Non-polar molecules** are usually soluble in **non-polar solvents** such as hexane, and tetrachloromethane, CCl_4.

- The more **polar** the molecule is, the more likely it is to dissolve in **polar** solvents such as water and the less likely it is to dissolve in non-polar solvents.

Put simply, 'like dissolves like'!

Therefore, to answer the question above, you need to know that ethanol and water are both polar, and so ethanol will be soluble in water.

5 Picking up Points in Problem Solving

General Advice

Flow diagrams

Drawing chemical apparatus

Chemistry in an unfamiliar context

Investigative techniques

Problem solving questions are often found difficult by students. They can be put off by a complicated diagram, an experimental technique they have never heard of, or by unfamiliar chemical compounds. The key to success in these questions is to practise as many as you can, don't be nervous about having a go and see them as an achievable challenge, not an insurmountable obstacle.

GENERAL ADVICE

Problem solving questions come in a variety of styles. They range from the analysis of flow diagrams, the completion and drawing of apparatus, chemistry in an unfamiliar context and, towards the end of the paper, questions based on techniques you will not have met as part of the Higher course.

When tackling these types of questions, you should take the following approach:

- Read the question at least twice.
- Before answering each part of the question, it is much better to read through the whole question to determine what it is about. Often one part of a question follows on from another, and this can give you an idea of exactly what is wanted.
- Then read through the specific question you want to answer and underline or highlight the important instructions.

Flow diagrams

These questions describe the different steps involved in the industrial manufacture of an element or compound. Various types of reaction will be used during the manufacturing process. Typical examples of the type of chemical reactions involved are neutralisation, precipitation and displacement. You will have already met these as part of the Standard Grade or Intermediate 2 course.

If the industrial process involves organic compounds, then reactions such as oxidation, hydrolysis, condensation and addition are frequently employed.

Also several separation techniques or processes may be used, such as distillation (when the compounds have different boiling points) or filtration (separation of a solid from a liquid).

EXAMPLES

So, how do we answer questions involving flow diagrams?

Example 1

SQA Section B 2007 Q7

Magnesium metal can be extracted from sea water. An outline of the reactions involved is shown in the flow diagram.

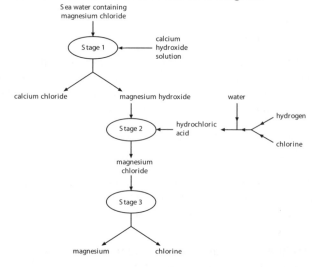

a. Why can the magnesium hydroxide be easily separated from the calcium chloride at stage 1?

b. Name the type of reaction taking place at stage 2.

c. Give **two** features of this process that make it economical.

Solution

a. The term 'easily separated' provides the clue to answering the question. It suggests that perhaps a simple technique could be used to separate them. The first thing to consider would be the solubilities of calcium chloride and magnesium hydroxide.

   If we turn to the data booklet we see that magnesium hydroxide is insoluble in water, whereas calcium chloride is very soluble in water. Because of this difference in solubility, they can be easily separated

b. The reaction of a base with an acid is **neutralisation**. (Remember that a base is any chemical which will accept H^+ ions.)

c. When asked what features make a process economical (as covered in the Chemical Industry topic), then we should be considering the following:

   i. *Are any chemicals recycled in the process?*

      Inspection of the diagram shows that the chlorine produced as a result of stage 3 can be used in the production of the hydrochloric acid which is used in stage 2.

   ii. *What is the cost of raw materials?*

      The process uses sea water which is cheap and plentiful.

Example

SQA Section B 2006 Q7

An industrial method for the production of ethanol is outlined in the flow diagram.

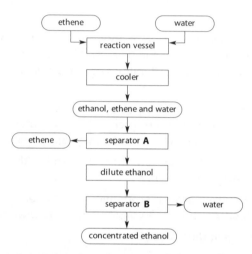

a. Name the type of chemical reaction that takes place in the reaction vessel. **1 mark**

b. Unreacted ethene is removed in separator **A**.
   Suggest how the separated ethene could be used to increase the efficiency of the overall process. **1 mark**

c. Name the process that takes place in separator **B**.

Solution

a. **Addition**
   Alkenes always undergo addition reactions. The reaction of ethene and water is also known as **hydration**. Both answers are acceptable.

b. To increase the efficiency of the process the ethene removed from separator A would be recycled back into the reaction vessel.

c. The process is **distillation**. The separation is based on the fact that ethanol and water have different boiling points.

DRAWING CHEMICAL APPARATUS

Drawing labelled diagrams of apparatus is a very good way of proving that you understand the concepts behind the experiments. The most important things to remember here are:

- draw your diagram carefully and clearly
- label up each key piece of apparatus
- make sure your diagram will work: don't block off an area where gas should be flowing through

Example

SQA Section B 2006 Q13(a)

When a mixture of solid sodium hydroxide and solid sodium ethanoate is heated, methane gas and solid sodium carbonate are produced.

$$NaOH(s) + CH_3COONa(s) \rightarrow CH_4(g) + Na_2CO_3(s)$$

Draw a diagram of apparatus which could be used for this reaction showing how the methane gas can be collected and its volume measured.

(2 marks)

Solution

The first mark is for the heating of the sodium hydroxide and sodium ethanoate mixture. This is done by placing the reactants in a test tube, attaching a delivery tube and heating with a bunsen burner.

The second mark is for the collection and measurement of the gas. We have two options: either use a graduated gas syringe or collect the gas over water using an inverted measuring cylinder filled with water. If you use a test tube to collect the gas then you cannot measure the volume and you would lose a ½ mark.

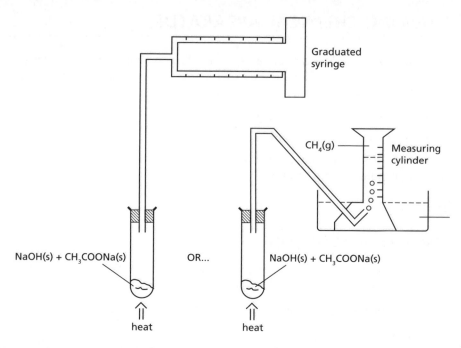

NaOH(s) + CH₃COONa(s) → $NaOH(s) + CH_3COONa(s)$

OR...

heat   heat

Example

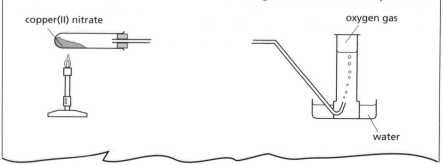

Solution

At temperatures below 22°C nitrogen dioxide would become a liquid while oxygen with a boiling point of –183°C would remain as a gas. So, to separate gases with different boiling points all we need to do is cool the gases down. We do this by placing the delivery tube in a beaker containing ice.

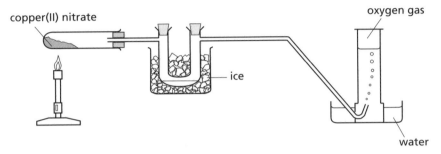

CHEMISTRY IN AN UNFAMILIAR CONTEXT

Quite often these questions are linked to Unit 2 work, that is, organic chemistry. To help us answer them, let's remind ourselves of the functional groups we need to know.

Functional group	Name
—C=C—	carbon-to-carbon double bond
—C≡C—	carbon-to-carbon triple bond
—O—H	hydroxyl group
H | —C=O	carbonyl group (aldehydes)
O || —C—	carbonyl group (ketones)
O || —C—O—H	carboxyl group

Functional group	Name
O || —C—O—	ester link
O H || | —C—N—	amide/peptide link
H / —N \\ H	amino
⬡	phenyl

Example

SQA Section B 2000 Q14

Alkanols can be prepared by the reaction of carbonyl compounds with methyl magnesium bromide. The reaction takes place in two stages.

Stage 1

Methyl magnesium bromide reacts with methanal in an addition reaction across the double bond.

methanal   methyl magnesium bromide

Stage 2

Reaction of the product with water produces ethanol.

ethanol

a. Suggest a name for the type of reaction which takes place in **stage 2**.

b. Draw a structural product if propanone had been used in place of methanal.

Solution

a. The unwary candidate may look at this too quickly and answer 'hydration'. However this would be wrong! If we look closely we see that the reactant molecule is being broken up by the addition of water into two product molecules. The breaking up of a molecule into two product molecules means that the type of reaction taking place is hydrolysis.

The term *lysis* comes from the Greek meaning 'to break up'. The ending 'lysis' regularly appears in chemistry, for example, electro*lysis*, which is the breaking up of a compound using electricity.

It is important you do not confuse hydrolysis with hydration. Both involve water as reactant. However, with hydration the water **adds** on to the reactant to form only **one** product molecule, whereas with hydrolysis the reactant is **broken up** into **two** product molecules.

b. Both methanal and propanone contain the same functional group, that is, the carbonyl group

$$\begin{array}{c} \diagdown \\ \diagup \end{array} C = O$$

It is important you realise that the functional group is the site of reaction. Therefore, in questions of this type, this is the part of the molecule you should be focusing on.

The stem of the question tells us that the methyl magnesium bromide reacts with methanal in an addition reaction across the double bond. Careful examination of the stage 1 reaction shows us that the methyl group, CH_3, of the methyl magnesium bromide is adding to the carbon atom of the functional group and the MgBr is being added to the oxygen atom of the functional group.

The same pattern should apply when we use propanone in place of methanal. It is also helpful to draw propanone in a similar fashion showing the functional group facing the methyl magnesium bromide.

Stage 1:

$$\underset{\text{propanone}}{\overset{H_3C}{\underset{H_3C}{\diagdown}}C=O} + \underset{\substack{\text{methyl} \\ \text{magnesium} \\ \text{bromide}}}{\overset{H}{\underset{H}{H-\overset{|}{\underset{|}{C}}-MgBr}}} \longrightarrow H-\overset{\overset{H}{|}}{\underset{\underset{H}{|}}{C}}-\overset{\overset{CH_3}{|}}{\underset{\underset{CH_3}{|}}{C}}-O-MgBr$$

The structure of the product now mirrors what was taking place when the methyl magnesium bromide was being added to methanal.

Stage 2: this part of the reaction is much more straightforward. The O—MgBr bond is broken with a hydrogen from water being added to the oxygen atom as shown.

$$H{-}\overset{\displaystyle H}{\underset{\displaystyle H}{C}}{-}\overset{\displaystyle CH_3}{\underset{\displaystyle CH_3}{C}}{-}O{-}MgBr + H_2O \longrightarrow H{-}\overset{\displaystyle H}{\underset{\displaystyle H}{C}}{-}\overset{\displaystyle CH_3}{\underset{\displaystyle CH_3}{C}}{-}OH + MgBrOH$$

Therefore the structural formula for the alcohol if propanone had been used is:

$$H{-}\overset{\displaystyle H}{\underset{\displaystyle H}{C}}{-}\overset{\displaystyle CH_3}{\underset{\displaystyle CH_3}{C}}{-}OH$$

Example

SQA Section B 2000 Q11

Peeled apples turn brown due to the reactions of compounds called phenols.

The first two steps in the reaction of one phenol, **A**, are:

a. Write the molecular formula for compound **A**.

b. The same type of reaction takes place in both steps.
   Give the name of this type of reaction.

Solution

a. The formula for benzene is C_6H_6. However, two of the hydrogen atoms in the structure have been replaced with an OH group and a CH_3 group. This means the molecular formula is C_7H_8O. The order of the atoms is not important. You could easily have written H_8C_7O and still be awarded the mark. However, if you answer $C_6H_4OHCH_3$ then you would be marked wrong because this is not a molecular formula but in fact a shortened structural formula.

b. If you look at the middle molecule you can see it contains the hydroxyl group (–O–H). One of the key reactions you have to know in Unit 2 is that an alcohol can be oxidised to an aldehyde or ketone. Aldehydes and ketones both contain the carbonyl group. The molecule at the end of the sequence contains the carbonyl group ($C=O$). Therefore the molecule has undergone an oxidation reaction.

Can you think of another way to check that your answer is correct?

With an oxidation reaction the oxygen to hydrogen ratio increases, which you can check simply by counting the atoms present.

 In the examples given above we have shown how important it is to be able to recognise the functional groups. It is well worth your while to learn them!

Example

> ### SQA Section B 2006 Q12(b)
>
> The enthalpy change for the reaction
>
> $$K(s) + \tfrac{1}{2}Cl_2(g) + 1\tfrac{1}{2}O_2(g) \rightarrow KClO_3(s)$$
>
> is an example of an enthalpy of formation.
>
> The enthalpy of formation of a compound can be defined as the enthalpy change for the formation of one mole of a compound from its elements as they exist at room temperature.
>
> Write the equation, including state symbols, corresponding to the enthalpy of formation of sodium oxide (Na_2O).

Solution

The enthalpy of formation is not something you will have met as part of the Higher Course. You don't need to worry, though, because the question provides you with all the information required, and you have been given an example equation.

When you read through the stem of the question, you will see that the key piece of information is that the enthalpy of formation is defined as **the formation of one mole of the compound from its elements as they exist at room temperature**.

You are simply being asked to write a balanced chemical equation for the formation of one mole of sodium oxide (you are given the formula) showing state symbols.

The equation for the enthalpy of formation of sodium oxide is therefore

$2Na(s) + \frac{1}{2}O_2(g) \rightarrow Na_2O(s)$

Example

SQA Section B 2000 Q17

Chlorine can be manufactured by different industrial processes.

In the Castner-Kellner cell, chlorine is made by the electrolysis of brine (sodium chloride solution).

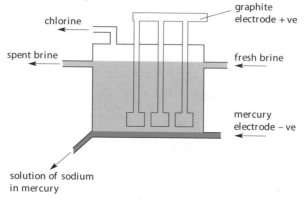

a. Why is graphite able to conduct electricity?

b. In the above process, the solution of sodium in mercury is treated with water to give two useful products. Name these **two** products.

Solution

a. This is a straightforward question. Carbon conducts because it has delocalised electrons.

b. Here you have to realise that only very reactive metals will react with cold water.

Sodium metal will react with cold water giving sodium hydroxide solution and hydrogen gas:

$Na(s) + H_2O(\ell) \rightarrow NaOH(aq) + H_2(g)$.

The mercury mixed with the sodium will not react with the cold water. Therefore the two products are **sodium hydroxide solution** and **hydrogen gas**.

INVESTIGATIVE TECHNIQUES

If you have been using practice papers to aid your revision (which you should definitely have been doing), then you will have come across these questions near the end of the papers. Although the chemistry is brand new, do not panic! You are not expected to have any prior understanding – you will be told everything you need to know within the question. Let's look at one example to show you that these questions are very do-able!

Example

> ### SQA Section B 2006 Q16
>
> Infrared spectroscopy can be used to help identify the bonds which are present in an organic molecule.
>
> Different bonds absorb infrared radiation of different wave numbers.
>
> The table below shows the range of wave numbers of infrared radiation absorbed by the bonds indicated with thicker lines.
>
> | Bond | Wave number range/cm⁻¹ |
> |:---:|:---:|
> | C━H | 3650 – 3590 |
> | C≡C━H | 3300 |
> | C—C━H | 2962 – 2853 |
> | C≡C | 2260 – 2100 |
> | C━O | 1150 – 1070 |
>
> The infrared spectrum and full structural formula for compound 1 are shown.
>
>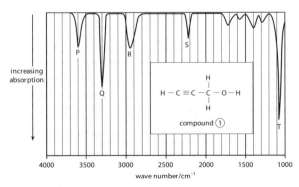

a. Identify the bond that could be responsible for the absorption at **T** in its infrared spectrum.

b. A series of reactions is carried out starting with compound 1.

$$\text{compound 1} \xrightarrow{\text{1 mol of } H_2} \text{compound 2} \xrightarrow{\text{1 mol of } H_2} \text{compound 3}$$

   i. Give the letters for the **two** absorptions which would **not** appear in the infrared spectrum for compound 2.

   ii. Name compound 3.

Solution

a. If you look at the infrared spectrum given for compound 1 you can see that **T** has a wave number of approximately 1100 cm⁻¹. Now refer to the table to determine which bond has a similar wave number. The **C–O** bond has a wave number range of 1150–1070 cm⁻¹. Therefore it is this bond which is responsible for the absorption at T.

b. i. The best way of tackling this part of the question is to draw out the structural formula for each compound involved in the reaction sequence. (Remember that you were given the structure of compound 1 in the question.) This will also help you to answer part (ii) of the question.

In the first reaction, hydrogen will add across the triple bond giving compound 2. Then hydrogen will add across the carbon-to-carbon double bond forming compound 3.

Compound 2 no longer has a C ≡ C triple bond; the wave number range for such bonds is 2260–2100 cm⁻¹. Looking at the spectrum, this corresponds to absorption **S**. Compound 2 no longer has a H—C≡C bond; the wave number range for this bond is 3300 cm⁻¹. If you look at the spectrum, this corresponds to absorption **Q**.

ii. From the structure seen above, you can clearly see that the compound is propan-1-ol.

6 Being Prepared for Prescribed Practical Activities (PPAs)

Section B of the exam contains questions worth six marks which are directly related to the PPAs. The Principal Assessor's Report has consistently stated that candidate achievement in the PPA questions is very disappointing.

The questions focus on the practical aspects of the PPAs – the names of chemicals/reagents used, what measurements were taken, observations made, sources of error, the drawing of relevant diagrams and being aware of the hazards. It is imperative that you spend time learning them in detail.

The following is a summary of the nine PPAs.

UNIT 1 — ENERGY MATTERS

Effect of concentration on the rate of a reaction

In acidic conditions, hydrogen peroxide reacts with iodide ions to form water and iodine:

$$H_2O_2(aq) + 2H^+(aq) + 2I^-(aq) \rightarrow 2H_2O(\ell) + I_2(aq) \quad \text{equation 1}$$

The course of the reaction can be followed by adding starch and thiosulphate solutions to the reaction mixture. The thiosulphate ion reacts with the iodine to produce iodide ions:

$$S_2O_3^{2-}(aq) + I_2(aq) \rightarrow 2I^-(aq) + S_4O_6^{2-}(aq) \qquad \text{equation 2}$$

When all the thiosulphate ions have reacted, a blue/black colour suddenly appears because the iodine produced in equation (1) is no longer being reduced into I^- ions (as in equation (2)) and so the iodine I_2 now reacts with the starch solution. The time taken, t, for the solution to turn from colourless to blue/black is measured in seconds and the reaction rate is calculated from 1/time. The units are s^{-1}.

You use the same volumes of all the other reactants, except potassium iodide. The concentration of the potassium iodide is changed by diluting it with water but keeping the same total volume each time.

- In carrying out the experiment, the temperature and the volumes of the other reactants must be kept constant.
- It is easy to measure the time taken for the reaction due to the sharp colour change.

Effect of temperature on the rate of a reaction

Oxalic acid $(COOH)_2$, reacts with acidified potassium permanganate solution.

$$5(COOH)_2(aq) + 6H^+(aq) + \underset{\text{purple}}{2MnO_4^{2-}(aq)} \rightarrow \underset{\text{colourless}}{2Mn^{2+}(aq)} + 8H_2O(\ell) + 10CO_2(g)$$

The reaction mixture is initially purple due to the MnO_4^{2-} ions but it will turn colourless as soon as they are used up.

The mixture of potassium permanganate, sulphuric acid and water is heated to approximately 40°C and placed on a white tile (this makes it easier to detect the colour change). Oxalic acid is added; the time, t, for the solution to turn from purple to colourless is measured in seconds; and the temperature of the solution is noted. Then the reaction rate is calculated from

$$\text{reaction rate} = \frac{1}{\text{time}} \quad \text{(units are s}^{-1}\text{)}$$

The above procedure is repeated at a selection of higher temperatures.

- Dry beakers are used when carrying out the experiment to ensure the concentrations and volumes of the reactants are kept constant.
- It is difficult to get an accurate reaction time if the experiment is carried out at temperatures below 30°C because the colour change is too gradual.

Enthalpy of combustion of ethanol

The enthalpy of combustion of ethanol is the energy released when one mole of ethanol is burned completely in oxygen.

$$C_2H_5OH(\ell) + 3O_2(g) \rightarrow 2CO_2(g) + 3H_2O(\ell)$$

A diagram of the apparatus used is shown below.

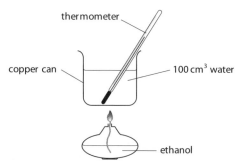

The following procedure is carried out.

The burner containing the ethanol is weighed then placed under the copper can. A known volume of water is added to the copper can and its temperature measured. The burner is then lit and, when the temperature of the water has risen by approximately 10°C, it is extinguished and reweighed. The highest temperature reached by the water is measured.

In summary, the following measurements were taken during the experiment:

- the initial and final mass of the burner containing the ethanol
- the volume of water added to the copper can
- the initial and final temperature of the water

The main sources of error are:

- incomplete combustion of the ethanol
- heat loss to the surroundings
- loss of ethanol through evaporation
- incomplete stirring

UNIT 2 — WORLD OF CARBON

Oxidation

Aldehydes and ketones are isomers – they have the same molecular formula but different structural formula. It is this difference in structure that enables aldehydes to undergo mild oxidation whereas ketones do not.

This PPA uses three different oxidising agents to distinguish between an aldehyde and a ketone. The table below summarises the results.

Oxidising agent	Observation with aldehyde	Observation with ketone
acidified dichromate solution	colour changes from **orange to green/blue**	no colour change
Fehling's solution	colour changes from **blue to brick red**	no colour change
Tollens' reagent	a **'silver mirror'** forms	no 'silver mirror' forms

- The reaction mixtures are heated using a hot water bath since both aldehydes and ketones are flammable.
- Aldehydes are oxidised to carboxylic acids.

   For example:

propanal → (oxidation) → propanoic acid

butanal → (oxidation) → butanoic acid

Making Esters

A labelled diagram of the assembled apparatus used to prepare an ester is shown below.

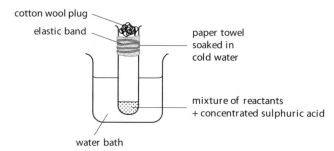

The alcohol and carboxylic acid are added to a test tube along with a few drops of concentrated sulphuric acid which is the catalyst for the reaction. A wet paper towel is wrapped around the neck of the test tube to act as a condenser, preventing loss of the volatile ester, alcohol and carboxylic acid.

A plug of cotton wool is inserted into the mouth of the test tube, after which it is then placed in the hot water bath. After a period of time, the mixture is carefully poured into a beaker of sodium hydrogencarbonate solution. This neutralises the catalyst and any remaining carboxylic acid. The ester separates from the aqueous mixture forming an oily layer on the surface. It has a pleasant smell.

- A hot water bath has to be used to heat the reaction mixture since the alcohol, carboxylic acid and ester are all flammable.
- The rate of the reaction is increased by heating in a water bath and using a catalyst (concentrated sulphuric acid).

The following equation shows the formation of an ester:

$$\underset{\text{ethanoic acid}}{\text{H—C—C—O—H}} + \underset{\text{propan-1-ol}}{\text{H—O—C—C—C—H}} \longrightarrow \underset{\text{propyl ethanoate}}{\text{H—C—C—O—C—C—C—H}} + H_2O$$

The reaction of an alcohol with a carboxylic acid to make an ester is an example of a **condensation** reaction – the joining of two molecules with the elimination of a small molecule which is usually, but not always, water.

Factors affecting enzyme activity

The enzyme catalase, found in potato, catalyses the decomposition of hydrogen peroxide into water and oxygen:

$$2H_2O_2(aq) \rightarrow 2H_2O(\ell) + O_2(g)$$

The aim of this PPA is to investigate the effect that changing either the pH or the temperature will have on enzyme activity. The activity of the enzyme is measured by counting the number of bubbles of oxygen gas produced in three minutes. The apparatus used is shown below.

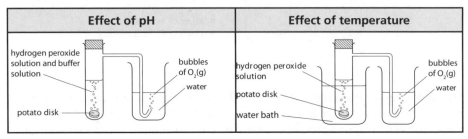

Effect of pH

5 cm³ of pH 7 buffer solution along with three potato disks is added to a test tube with a side arm and left for three minutes. 1 cm³ hydrogen peroxide solution is added and the number of oxygen bubbles produced in the first three minutes is recorded. The experiment is repeated using solutions of varying pH (1 ,4, 10 and 13).

- During this investigation, the potato disks are left to stand for three minutes in order to give the enzyme time to adjust to the pH.
- To ensure valid results, all other factors such as temperature, number of disks used and volume of solutions are kept constant.

Effect of temperature

5 cm³ of deionised water along with three potato disks are added to a test tube with a side arm. The test tube is then placed in a water bath at 30°C and left for three minutes. 1 cm³ hydrogen peroxide solution is added and the number of oxygen bubbles produced in three minutes is recorded. The experiment is repeated using temperatures of 40°C, 50°C and 60°C.

- During this investigation the potato discs are left to stand in the water bath for three minutes in order to give the enzyme time to adjust to the temperature.
- To ensure valid results, all other factors such as pH, number of discs used and volume of solutions are kept constant.

UNIT 3 – CHEMICAL REACTIONS

Hess's Law

This PPA is used to confirm Hess's Law which states that **the enthalpy change for a reaction is independent of the route taken**.

Solid potassium hydroxide can be converted into potassium chloride solution by two different routes.

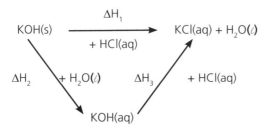

Route 1: Direct route (calculation of ΔH_1)

The temperature of a 25 cm³ HCl solution is measured. Solid KOH is then added to the acid and the maximum temperature reached recorded. The heat energy gained by the reaction mixture is calculated using $E_h = cm\Delta T$ and then the heat energy released for one mole of KOH is determined. This is ΔH_1.

Route 2: Indirect Route ($\Delta H_2 + \Delta H_3$)

The temperature of 25 cm³ water is measured. Solid KOH is then added to the water and the highest temperature reached recorded. The heat energy gained by the reaction mixture is calculated using $E_h = cm\Delta T$. The heat energy released for one mole of KOH is then determined. This is ΔH_2.

The temperature of the KOH solution just prepared is measured and the solution is then added to a 25 cm³ solution of HCl whose temperature is also known. The starting temperature is calculated as an average of the two solutions. The highest temperature reached by the reaction mixture is recorded.

The heat energy gained by the reaction mixture is calculated using $E_h = cm\Delta T$.

The heat energy released for one mole is then determined. This is ΔH_3.

Polystyrene cups and lids are used to reduce heat losses.

Quantitative Electrolysis

When dilute sulphuric acid $(H^+)_2SO_4^{2-}(aq)$, is electrolysed, H_2 gas is produced at the negative electrode. The ion-electron equation is:

$$2H^+(aq) + 2e^- \rightarrow H_2(g)$$

The aim of this PPA is to show that 193,000C is required to produce one mole of hydrogen gas. The apparatus used to carry out the experiment is shown below.

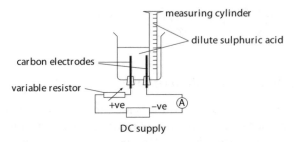

The circuit must include an ammeter and a variable resistor – this controls the current. The measuring cylinder is **not** placed over the negative electrode initially. The power supply is switched on and the variable resistor adjusted to give a current of 0·5 A. The current is allowed to pass through the solution for a few minutes. This allows the porous carbon electrodes to be completely saturated with hydrogen gas. The power is switched off and the measuring cylinder placed over the **negative electrode**. The power is switched on and, at the same time, a stop clock is started.

When approximately 50 cm³ of hydrogen gas have been collected, the power is switched off and the time recorded, together with the current and the exact volume of hydrogen gas collected.

The number of coulombs required to produce this volume of hydrogen gas is calculated using Q = It. The number of coulombs required to produce one mole of hydrogen can then be calculated.

Sources of error associated with this PPA are:

● the current was not constant

● an error in measuring the exact volume of hydrogen gas produced

A Redox Titration

The aim of this PPA is to determine the mass of vitamin C in a commercially produced tablet. Vitamin C undergoes a redox reaction with iodine; the vitamin C reduces the iodine to iodide ions.

The ion-electron equations taking place are:

$C_6H_8O_6 \rightarrow C_6H_6O_6 + 2H^+ + 2e^-$ oxidation

$I_2 + 2e^- \rightarrow 2I^-$ reduction

$\overline{C_6H_8O_6 + I_2 \rightarrow C_6H_6O_6 + 2I^-}$ balanced redox equation

Procedure

A vitamin C tablet is dissolved in 50 cm³ of deionised water and the solution plus washings are transferred to a 250 cm³ standard flask which is then made up to the mark with deionised water. The flask is inverted several times to ensure the solution is thoroughly mixed.

After rinsing the pipette with the vitamin C solution, 25 cm³ is pipetted into a conical flask and a few drops of starch indicator added. The burette is rinsed, then filled with the iodine solution. The iodine solution is added from the burette into the conical flask until a blue/black colour is obtained. The titration is repeated until two concordant results (within 0·1 cm³) are obtained.

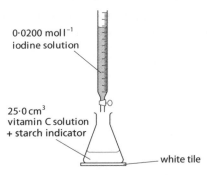

0·0200 mol l^{-1}
iodine solution

25·0 cm³
vitamin C solution
+ starch indicator

white tile

Calculation

Knowing the average volume and concentration of the iodine solution, the number of moles of iodine can be determined. Using the balanced redox equation, the number of moles of vitamin C in 25 cm³ can be determined.

To get the total number of moles of vitamin C in the tablet, multiply by 10 because the total volume of the vitamin C solution is 250 cm³. The mass of vitamin C present in the tablet is found by multiplying the number of moles by the Formula Mass of vitamin C.

PPA QUESTIONS

Example

> ### SQA Section B 2007 Q4 + 2008 Q9
>
> Hydrogen gas can be produced in the lab by the electrolysis of dilute sulphuric acid.
>
> a. Above which electrode should the measuring cylinder be placed to collect the hydrogen gas? **(1 mark)**
>
> b. In addition to the current, what other measurements should be taken? **(1 mark)**

Solution

   a. The **negative electrode**. All acids contain the H^+ ion – positively charged ions are attracted to the negative electrode. This would be marked as a 1 or 0.

   b. Straightforward recall required. The volume of H_2 gas and the time taken for this volume to be produced. (½ + ½)

Example

SQA Section B 2001 Q3

The effect of temperature changes on reaction rate can be studied using the reaction between an organic acid solution and acidified potassium permanganate solution.

$$5(COOH)_2(aq) + 6H^+(aq) + 2MnO_4^-(aq) \rightarrow Mn^{2+}(aq) + 10CO_2(g) + 8H_2O(\ell)$$

a. Name the organic acid.   **(1 mark)**

b. Describe how the reaction time can be measured.   **(1 mark)**

Solution

   a. It is **oxalic acid**.

   b. You measure the time taken for the solution to turn from purple to colourless.   **(1 or 0)**

Example

SQA Section B 2000 Q3

A student was studying the effect of varying the pH on the activity of catalase, an enzyme found in potatoes.

a. Draw a labelled diagram of the apparatus used.   **(1 mark)**

b. Describe how the enzyme activity was measured.   **(1 mark)**

Solution

   a. The diagram would be the same as that shown on page 102.

   b. The activity was measured by counting the number of bubbles in a fixed period of time, that is, 3 minutes. If you had just said 'by counting the bubbles' then you would get no mark.

General question

Ethyl pentanoate is an ester. It can be prepared in the laboratory as shown below.

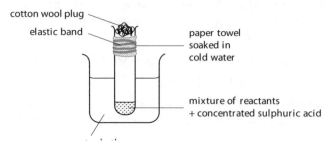

cotton wool plug

elastic band

paper towel
soaked in
cold water

mixture of reactants
+ concentrated sulphuric acid

a. Why is a water bath used for heating?   (1 mark)

b. What is the purpose of the wet paper towel?   (1 mark)

c. Name the catalyst used in the reaction.   (1 mark)

d. What evidence would show that an ester had formed?   (1 mark)

Solution

a. The water bath is used, instead of a bunsen burner, to reduce the risk of fire since the reactants and products are very flammable.

b. The wet paper towel acts as a condenser to ensure that none of the volatile reactants or products are allowed to escape into the atmosphere.

c. The catalyst used is **concentrated** sulphuric acid.(1 or 0). If you answer sulphuric acid then the mark will not be awarded. The PPA requires you to know that the sulphuric acid was concentrated.

d. Any one of the following answers would be acceptable: an oily layer forms on the surface, a separate layer on the surface or a pleasant smell is produced.

Example

Solution

'What is observed'? A 'silver mirror' would form on the sides of the test tube,
but this answer as it stands would only get you 1 mark. The question is worth 2
marks and is asking you to **explain** what is observed. Therefore a reference to the
theory of why a 'silver mirror' is formed is required for the second mark.

Tollen's reagent is a mild oxidising agent containing silver ions, $Ag^+(aq)$. When it
oxidises propanal, the Ag^+ ions are reduced to silver atoms:

$$Ag^+(aq) + e^- \rightarrow Ag(s)$$

It is the presence of the silver atoms which result in the 'silver mirror' being
formed.

Do You Know Your Definitions?

The Higher course is full of definitions. You could be asked to repeat any of these in an exam so you need to learn them off by heart. The following is a list of the definitions you could be asked. In some cases, some information is also provided to ensure that you really understand the Chemistry involved.

UNIT 1 — ENERGY MATTERS

The **activation energy** E_A – the minimum kinetic energy required by colliding particles before a reaction will occur.

Catalysts – increase the rate of a reaction by providing an alternative route for the reaction with a lower activation energy.

Heterogeneous catalyst – the catalyst is in a **different state to the reactants**.

Homogeneous catalyst – the catalyst is in the **same state as the reactants**.

Enthalpy changes

a. The **enthalpy of combustion** of a substance is the energy change when **one mole** of the substance burns completely in oxygen. These enthalpy values are always negative (exothermic).

$$CH_4(g) + 2O_2(g) \rightarrow CO_2(g) + 2H_2O(\ell)$$

b. The **enthalpy of solution** of a substance is the energy change when **one mole** of a substance dissolves in water. The enthalpy of solution can be exothermic or endothermic.

$$NaOH(s) + H_2O(\ell) \rightarrow Na^+(aq) + OH^-(aq)$$

c. The **enthalpy of neutralisation** of an acid is the energy change when the acid is neutralised to form **one mole** of water. These enthalpy values are always negative (endothermic).

$$H^+Cl^-(aq) + Na^+OH^-(aq) \rightarrow Na^+Cl^-(aq) + H_2O(\ell)$$

First ionisation energy – the energy required to remove one mole of electrons from one mole of gaseous atoms of the element

1st ionisation energy equation for magnesium: $Mg(g) \rightarrow Mg^+(g) + e^-$

Electronegativity – a measure of the attraction an atom involved in a bond has for the electrons of the bond

UNIT 2 — WORLD OF CARBON

Reforming – alters the arrangement of atoms in a hydrocarbon molecule without necessarily changing the number of carbon atoms in the molecule. As a result of the reforming process, straight chained alkanes are converted into branched, cyclic and aromatic hydrocarbons.

octane → 2,2,3-trimethylpentane

hexane → cyclohexane + H_2

Cracking – the breaking down of long chain hydrocarbons into shorter chained alkanes and alkenes. Heat and the catalyst aluminium oxide are used

$$C_8H_{18} \rightarrow C_4H_{10} + C_4H_8$$

Types of reactions

a. **Hydration** – the addition of water. Water can be represented as H—OH

propene → propan-1-ol

b. **Dehydration** – the removal of water

propan-1-ol → propene + H—OH

c. **Hydrolysis** – the breaking up of a molecule by the addition of water

$$
\begin{array}{l}
H_2C-O-\overset{\displaystyle O}{\overset{\|}{C}}-C_{17}H_{35} \\[2mm]
CH-O-\overset{\displaystyle O}{\overset{\|}{C}}-C_{17}H_{35} \;+\; H_2O \\[2mm]
H_2C-O-\overset{\displaystyle O}{\overset{\|}{C}}-C_{17}H_{35}
\end{array}
\quad\longrightarrow\quad
\begin{array}{l}
H_2C-O-H \\[2mm]
CH-O-H \;+\; 3\,HO-\overset{\displaystyle O}{\overset{\|}{C}}-C_{17}H_{35} \\[2mm]
H_2C-O-H
\end{array}
$$

fat   glycerol   fatty acid

d. **Condensation** – the joining of two molecules with the elimination of a small molecule (usually water)

$$
H_3C-\overset{\displaystyle O}{\overset{\|}{C}}-O-H \;+\; HO-CH_2-CH_3 \;\longrightarrow\; H_3C-\overset{\displaystyle O}{\overset{\|}{C}}-O-CH_2-CH_3 \;+\; H_2O
$$

e. **Hydrogenation** – addition of hydrogen

$$
\begin{array}{c}
H \\
| \\
H-C-C=C-H \;+\; H-H \\
| \;\;\; | \;\; | \\
H \;\; H \;\; H
\end{array}
\;\longrightarrow\;
\begin{array}{c}
H \;\; H \;\; H \\
| \;\; | \;\; | \\
H-C-C-C-H \\
| \;\; | \;\; | \\
H \;\; H \;\; H
\end{array}
$$

propene   propane

- Unsaturated oils can be saturated by the addition of hydrogen across the carbon-to-carbon double bonds in the presence of a nickel catalyst. This conversion of unsaturated oils into saturated fats is known as **hardening** and is used in the manufacture of margarine.

f. **Dehydrogenation** – the removal of hydrogen

$$
\begin{array}{c}
H \;\; H \;\; H \\
| \;\; | \;\; | \\
H-C-C-C-H \\
| \;\; | \;\; | \\
H \;\; H \;\; H
\end{array}
\;\longrightarrow\;
\begin{array}{c}
H \\
| \\
H-C-C=C-H \;+\; H-H \\
| \;\;\; | \;\; | \\
H \;\; H \;\; H
\end{array}
$$

propane   propene

g. **Polymerisation**

   i. **Addition** – the monomers contain the carbon-to-carbon double bond (C=C). Using the C=C as the starting point, you arrange the monomer to form an 'H' shape

$$
\begin{array}{c}
H \\
| \\
H-C-C=C-H \\
| \;\; | \;\; | \\
H \;\; H \;\; H
\end{array}
\;\longrightarrow\;
\begin{array}{c}
CH_3 \; H \\
| \;\; | \\
C=C \\
| \;\; | \\
H \;\; H
\end{array}
\;+\;
\begin{array}{c}
CH_3 \; H \\
| \;\; | \\
C=C \\
| \;\; | \\
H \;\; H
\end{array}
\;+\;
\begin{array}{c}
CH_3 \; H \\
| \;\; | \\
C=C \\
| \;\; | \\
H \;\; H
\end{array}
$$

propene   propene

$$\downarrow$$

$$
- - -\overset{\displaystyle CH_3}{\underset{\displaystyle H}{C}}-\overset{\displaystyle H}{\underset{\displaystyle H}{C}}-\overset{\displaystyle CH_3}{\underset{\displaystyle H}{C}}-\overset{\displaystyle H}{\underset{\displaystyle H}{C}}-\overset{\displaystyle CH_3}{\underset{\displaystyle H}{C}}-\overset{\displaystyle H}{\underset{\displaystyle H}{C}}- - -
$$

section of poly(propene)

ii. **Condensation** – each monomer must contain at least **two** functional groups, which allows the reaction to take place at both ends. The presence of ester bonds, amide bonds or peptide bonds in the structure of a polymer allows you to recognise it as a condensation polymer. (Polyesters, polyamides and proteins are examples of condensation polymers). Amino acids are the monomers used to make proteins.

amino acid

section of a protein

Remember to show the continuation at each end of the polymers.

h. **Oxidation** when applied to carbon compounds results in:
   – the gain of oxygen or loss of hydrogen
   – an increase in the oxygen to hydrogen ratio

i. **Reduction** when applied to carbon compounds results in:
   – the loss of oxygen or gain of hydrogen
   – a decrease in the oxygen to hydrogen ratio

UNIT 3 — CHEMICAL REACTIONS

a. **Hess's law** – states that the enthalpy change for a chemical reaction is independent of the route taken.

b. **At equilibrium** – the rate of the forward reaction is equal to the rate of the reverse reaction.

   – the concentrations of the reactants and products remains constant, although not necessarily equal

c. **Oxidation** – loss of electrons $Zn(s) \rightarrow Zn^{2+}(aq) + 2e^-$

d. **Reduction** – gain of electrons $Cl_2(g) + 2e^- \rightarrow 2Cl^-(aq)$

e. **Redox** – when both oxidation and reduction reactions take place

f. An **oxidising agent** is a substance which accepts electrons and is itself reduced. If you turn to the data book page 11, examples of oxidising agents can be found on the left hand side of the Standard Reduction Potential Table. For example, $H^+(aq)$, $Ag^+(aq)$, acidified dichromate $H^+/Cr_2O_7^{2-}$ and $Cl_2(g)$.

g. A **reducing agent** is a substance which loses electrons and is itself oxidised. Examples of reducing agents can be found on the right hand side of the Standard Reduction Potential Table, for example, $Mg(s)$, $SO_3^{2-}(aq)$, $I^-(aq)$.

h. **Half-life** – the time taken for the mass or activity of a radioisotope to halve

    – it is independent of the mass of isotope or its chemical state

    – it is not affected by changes in temperature or pressure

i. **Strong acids** are completely dissociated in aqueous solution

$$HCl(g) + H_2O \rightarrow H^+(aq) + Cl^-(aq)$$

A solution of hydrogen chloride contains **only** hydrogen ions and chloride ions.

Weak acids are only partially ionised in aqueous solution:

$$CH_3COOH\ (aq) \rightleftharpoons CH_3COO^-\ (aq) + H^+(aq)$$

Note the reversible sign – a solution of ethanoic acid contains a mixture of ethanoic acid molecules, hydrogen ions and ethanoate ions.

The same definitions apply to strong and weak bases.

 Make sure you know which acids and bases are strong and which ones are weak. Remember that page 12 of the data booklet has a list of weak acids.

j. **pH of salt solutions** – the pH of a salt solution depends on the acid and base used to prepare it. The table below is a reminder.

Acid	Base	pH of salt solution
strong	strong	equal to 7
strong	weak	less than 7
weak	strong	greater than 7

EXAMPLES OF EXTENDED ANSWER QUESTIONS

Questions based on definitions tend to be one mark questions with not much room for error! However, there are also a few extended answer question-types which it would be good to look at within this chapter.

Example

> ### SQA 2007 Section B Q1(a)
>
> What term is used as a measure of the attraction an atom involved in a bond has for the electrons of the bond? **(1 mark)**

Solution

Electronegativity – an easy 1 mark if we know our definitions.

Example

> Write the equation, showing state symbols, for the third ionisation energy for aluminium. **(1 mark)**

Solution

The equation is $Al^{2+}(g) \rightarrow Al^{3+}(g) + e^-$.

The units for ionisation energies are kJ mol^{-1}, that is, the energy required to remove one mole of electrons. Therefore, for each ionisation only one mole of electrons are removed each time.

This would be marked as 1 or 0. Even if the charges on the ions are correct, if you have not included the state symbols, then no marks would be awarded.

Example

SQA 2009 Section A Q23

What organic compound is produced by the dehydration of ethanol?

A Ethane

B Ethene

C Ethanal

D Ethanoic acid

Solution

Dehydration means to remove water. Ethanol is an alcohol and the removal of water from ethanol results in the alkene, ethene, being formed. The correct answer is **B**.

Example

SQA 2008 Section A Q 38

In which of the following reactions is the hydrogen ion acting as an oxidising agent?

A $Mg + 2HCl \rightarrow MgCl_2 + H_2$

B $NaOH + HNO_3 \rightarrow NaNO_3 + H_2O$

C $CuCO_3 + H_2SO_4 \rightarrow CuSO_4 + H_2O + CO_2$

D $CH_3COONa + HCl \rightarrow NaCl + CH_3COOH$

Solution

We know that an oxidising agent accepts electrons and examples of oxidising agents can be found on the left hand side of the Standard Reduction Potential table, page 11 of the data book. Looking at the table we can see the hydrogen ion, $H^+(aq)$, half way down on the left hand side.

The $H^+(aq)$ ion is accepting electrons and has been reduced to hydrogen gas:

$$2H^+(aq) + 2e^- \rightarrow H_2(g)$$

The only reaction showing hydrogen gas as a product is A, therefore **A** must be the correct answer.

Here is a question which looks very straightforward, but actually requires a bit more detail to get the full credit.

Example

> ### SQA 2007 Section B Q6(b)
>
> Why does a small increase in temperature produce a large increase in reaction rate? **(1 mark)**

Solution

If you simply said that there would be 'more collisions', then no marks would be awarded. If you said 'more **successful** collisions', this would be worth a ½ mark. To get the full mark, you have to state that more particles now have an energy greater than or equal to the activation energy E_a and therefore there is a greater chance of more successful collisions.

Example

> ### SQA 2004 Section B Q15(b)
>
> Ethanoic acid can be used to prepare the salt, sodium ethanoate, CH_3COONa.
>
> Explain why sodium ethanoate solution has a pH greater than 7.
>
> In your answer you should mention the **two** equilibria involved. **(3 marks)**

Solution

Simply stating that sodium ethanoate is the salt of a weak acid and strong base is not sufficient and would only get 1 mark. The question says **explain** and that you should include the two equilibria involved.

The two equilibria required are the equilibrium present in water:

$$H_2O(\ell) \rightleftharpoons H^+(aq) + OH^-(aq)$$

and the equilibrium present in ethanoic acid:

$$CH_3COOH(aq) \rightleftharpoons CH_3COO^-(aq) + H^+(aq)$$

To obtain full marks you should set out your answer as follows:

$$H_2O(\ell) \rightleftharpoons \quad H^+(aq) \quad + \quad OH^-(aq)$$

$$+$$

$$CH_3COONa(s) \quad \rightarrow \quad CH_3COO^-(aq) \quad + \quad Na^+(aq)$$

sodium ethanoate

$$\Updownarrow$$

$$CH_3COOH(aq)$$

When sodium ethanoate is added to water, the resulting ethanoate ions, CH_3COO^-, react with the hydrogen ions from the water forming ethanoic acid molecules, CH_3COOH. This effectively removes some of the hydrogen ions, resulting in the water equilibrium shifting to the right. This produces an excess of hydroxide ions, meaning the pH is greater than 7.

8 Now You're On Your Own!

Well, hopefully this book has been a helpful and interesting aid to your studies of Chemistry. Our aim was to give you an insight into the areas of the exam which pupils find most difficult and which are answered most poorly; and then to help you become better at these very areas. Through reading the text and practising the questions included, you should find that you are building a skill set which will support the work you are doing in your Higher class. However, we cannot leave you without imparting a little wisdom to help you be the best prepared you can for your exam.

DO

- Read each question carefully and make sure you answer what is asked.

- Use the number of marks awarded to each question to gauge how much detail is needed in your answer.

- A few words of explanation in your calculations can be a valuable aid in showing your thought processes. (Remember the examiner wants to give you marks.)

- Make sure your writing and presentation of your answer is clear and methodical; particularly in calculation questions.

- Keep an eye on your time. There are 1½ minutes allocated for each mark; keep that in mind and don't go too fast.

DON'T

- Feel the need to fill up every space on the paper – some people will have bigger writing than you!

- Give more information than is necessary. A two mark written question will generally require two full points. There is a danger that if you write too much in your answer you may contradict yourself and end up losing marks.

- Write out the question again – this is just a waste of time.

- Get tied up in a question you find hard, particularly in the Multiple Choice. These questions are only worth one mark and are not worth you fretting over them. Move on, and make sure you leave yourself time to do the extended questions.

- Forget to read your answers and check they make sense.

And the most important thing...

Good Luck!